CONVICTIONS THAT GIVE YOU CONFIDENCE

POTENTIALS
GUIDES FOR PRODUCTIVE LIVING

Wayne E. Oates, General Editor

CONVICTIONS THAT GIVE YOU CONFIDENCE

by

WAYNE E. OATES

THE WESTMINSTER PRESS
Philadelphia

Book design by Alice Derr

First edition

Published by The Westminster Press®
Philadelphia, Pennsylvania

PRINTED IN THE UNITED STATES OF AMERICA
2 4 6 8 9 7 5 3 1

Library of Congress Cataloging in Publication Data

Oates, Wayne Edward, 1917–
Convictions that give you confidence.

(Potentials)
1. Christian life—1960– . 2. Faith. 3. Confidence. I. Title. II. Series.
BV4501.2.O228 1984 248.4 84-5193
ISBN 0-664-24529-3 (pbk.)

To

Mary and Clarence Barton
Jackie and Walter Jackson
Judith and Andrew Lester
Jodi and Wade Rowatt
Betty and Edward Thornton

with
lasting gratitude
and
steadfast love

Contents

Foreword

The eleven books in this series, Potentials: Guides for Productive Living, speak to your condition and mine in the life we have to live today. The books are designed to ferret out the potentials you have with which to rise above rampant social and psychological problems faced by large numbers of individuals and groups. The purpose of rising above the problems is portrayed as far more than merely your own survival, merely coping, and merely "succeeding" while others fail. These books with one voice encourage you to save your own life by living with commitment to Jesus Christ, and to be a creative servant of the common good as well as your own good.

In this sense, the books are handbooks of ministry with a new emphasis: coupling your own well-being with the well-being of your neighbor. You use the tools of comfort wherewith God comforts you to be a source of strength to those around you. A conscious effort has been made by each author to keep these two dimensions of the second great commandment of our Lord Jesus Christ in harmony with each other.

The two great commandments are summarized in Luke 10:25–28: "And behold, a lawyer stood up to put him to the test, saying, 'Teacher, what shall I do to inherit eternal life?' He said to him, 'What is written in the law? How do you read?' And he answered, 'You shall love the Lord your God with all your heart, and with all your soul, and with all your strength, and with all your mind; and your neighbor as yourself.' And he said to him, 'You have answered right; do this, and you will live.' "

Underneath the two dimensions of neighbor and self there is also a persistent theme: The only way you can receive such harmony of thought and action is by the intentional re-centering of your life on the sovereignty of God and the rapid rejection of all idols that would enslave you. The theme, then, of this series of books is that these words of Jesus are the master guides both to the realization of your own potentials and to productive living in the nitty-gritty of your day's work.

The books in this series are unique, and each claims your attention separately in several ways.

First, these books address great social issues of our day, but they do so in terms of your own personal involvement in and responses to the problems. For example, the general problem of the public school system, the waste in American consumerism, the health hazards in a lack of rest and vocational burnout, the crippling effects of a defective mental outlook, and the incursion of Eastern mystical traditions into Western Christian activism are all larger-than-life issues. Yet each author translates the problem into the terms of day-to-day living and gives concrete guidelines as to what you can do about the problem.

Second, these books address the undercurrent of helplessness that overwhelming epidemic problems produce in you. The authors visualize you throwing up your hands and saying, "There is nothing *anyone* can do about it." Then they show you that this is not so, and that there are things *you* can do about it.

Third, the authors have all disciplined themselves to stay off their own soapboxes and to limit oratory about how awful the world is. They refuse to stop at gloomy diagnoses of incurable conditions. They go on to deal with your potentials for changing yourself and your world in very specific ways. They do not let you, the reader, off the hook with vague global utterances and generalized sermons. They energize you with a sense of hope that is generated by basic information, clear decision-making, and new directions taken by you yourself.

Fourth, these books get their basic interpretations and recommendations from a careful plumbing of the depths of the power of faith in God through Jesus Christ. They are not books that leave you with the illusion that you can lift yourself and your world by pulling hard at your own bootstraps. They energize and inspire you through the hope and strength that God in Christ is making available to you through the wisdom of the Bible and the presence of the living Christ in your life. Not even this, though, is presented in a namby-pamby or trite way. You will be surprised with joy at the freshness of the applications of biblical truths which you have looked at so often that you no longer notice their meaning. You will do many "double takes" with reference to your Bible as you read these books. You will find that the Bread of Life is not too holy or too good for human nature's daily food.

This present volume addresses the crisis of confidence in ourselves as individuals, groups, and a nation. It focuses this lack of confidence on the uncertainty of our convictions. The word "convictions" is used here in its positive sense, as beliefs that you have personally chosen, lay great store by, and according to which you live your daily life. These provide the beams and bolts that hold together the structure of your integrity as a person. They sustain you when trouble comes your way and keep your head on straight when you have successes and good fortune.

Furthermore, I emphasize that these convictions are hammered out on the anvil of experience in laborious encounter with the Creator. They are not inherited, although your heritage may have given them long-range nourishment. They are not handed to you by reason of position, status, or social class. They are not assured just because you have a formal education or denied because you do not have such training. They are wrought out of your deciding to forgo the luxury of indecision, by your working them out in your own personal wilderness, by your choosing whom you will serve, by your arriving at God's one clear calling for you, and by your deciding upon your own personal ethical code. May this book be something of a road map for you in these tasks!

WAYNE E. OATES

Louisville, Kentucky

Chapter 1

On the Fence or On Your Way?

For the last ten years I have been working in an inner-city emergency psychiatric clinic in my hometown. I teach in the clinic, coaching pastoral counseling residents, psychiatric residents, and junior and senior medical students. We meet persons who are trying to find their way and to build new foundations for their lives. They are all ages and come from all levels of poverty and privilege. They reflect intense versions of the same human concerns held by people like you and me and the people we meet in shops, offices, factories, churches, schools, and at home. As William James said, "There is only a little difference between human beings, but we make a whole lot out of what little differences there are."

One of the most satisfying aspects of my work is the important lessons I learn from the severely hurt and desperate persons with whom I converse. One man said to me, about another patient who was shaky, indecisive, frightened, "Jason is a good man, but he is not sure of his own judgment." He seemed to feel that Jason *had* convictions and that his inner terror came from his uncertainty about them. Shakespeare described this universal human condition well. He spoke in *Hamlet* of the "puzzled will" and the dread that "makes us rather bear those ills we have than fly to others we know not of. . . . Thus conscience does make cowards of us all; and thus the native hue of resolution is sicklied o'er with the pale cast of thought, and enterprises of great pith and moment . . . turn awry, and lose the name of action."

The crucial concern I want to discuss with you in this book is your and my personal confidence in the things we believe. You have convictions. Do you trust your own judgment enough to translate these beliefs into actions? That is the central issue of this book. Convictions held without confidence leave you shaken with fear and indecisive about your way of action.

Let me join you in a caution, which you may already be feeling. Not all people *seem* to lack confidence in their views about life. Some people seem so sure about what they think that they bully others and shove them around. Do they protest too loudly? They seem to be shouting to drown out their uncertainty. Surely we don't want to intimidate other people or whip them into line with our dogmatic teachings.

On the other hand, you and I also wonder with equal puzzlement about a larger group than those who never seem to lack confidence: the people who seem to have few convictions, if any, and are uncertain about those they do have. In fact, in America today, where we think another person's opinion is to be respected, where the right to hold a variety of convictions is both the law of the land and the daily assumption of our democracy, *to have firm beliefs and convictions is taboo.* And to translate such beliefs into action is to go against the party line, to stick out like a sore thumb, to seem just a wee bit unusual. Freedom of religion and freedom of speech can lead to a world in which any old belief is O.K. In behavior, anything goes. "Doing one's own thing" disregards responsibly taking a stand for personal beliefs that will hold you together. The pull and tug of the scores of varying life-styles shown in newspapers and magazines, and on radio and television, leave you confused. You need a clear path of action in which you believe wholeheartedly and from which you can draw personal serenity.

So, then, *not* to have convictions that give you confidence can *become* an issue for which you fight fiercely. Andras Angyal puts it bluntly when he describes a person who "refuses to take responsibility in identifying himself with his own actions. . . . He leads a brave fight for personal freedom, but since he does not use it when he has it the fight turns out to be a fight for the freedom to sit on the fence" (pp. 187–189; see Selected Bibliography for the full reference for this and other quoted material).

On the Fence: Indecision

Much of our lack of certainty in facing life comes from sitting on the fence of indecision. We say of a problem we can't make a clear decision about, "I'll sit on it for a while." This leaves unanswered the question, "How *long* will I sit on it?" To make a decision as to exactly *when* you will decide is the beginning of assurance, the seedling of confidence. An endless sitting on major commitments makes indecision a way of life.

The basic question you and I face as we sit on the fence of indecision is, "What are the forces in our lives that keep us on the fence?" Let me illustrate several. As I draw these word pictures, see if you fit into one or more of them. Bear in mind all the while that choosing personal principles that give you confidence is delicately tied to your dealings with other people throughout your personal history and with your meaningful—or not so meaningful—associates around you.

A conviction is, by definition, a strong belief formed on

the grounds of satisfying reasons or evidence you choose no longer to deny. A conviction is shaped by your capacity to trust yourself, those around you, and God. What then can keep you from reaching such a quiet depth of personal peace?

Too Many Options

A first reason you find yourself sitting on the fence is the infinite variety of beliefs being taught around you. You hold tight to the fence as the winds of doctrine try to toss you to and fro. This bewildering variety does not suddenly destroy your confidence as to which is *for you.* No, it subtly erodes your certainty that the differences between beliefs really matter. All these beliefs, contradictory as they may be, are held by sincere people. Maybe they are *all* right. Why choose where you yourself stand? You may find this is true in interfaith marriages of which you, your loved ones, or your friends are a part. Have you noticed that combining different faiths can result not in conflict but in neutrality? Often *neither* person's commitment matters.

The variety of beliefs and convictions prompts you to sit on the fence of indecision and agree superficially with all of them, holding none with any distinctness lest you seem dogmatic. When asked what you yourself have chosen to live by, you may say, "There is some truth in all religious and political beliefs, but *I am not anything.*" When you are intimidated by the competing convictions of others, you have a God-given right to examine your own life, arrive at your own convictions, and by them let it be known that *you are something.* Respecting other people's convictions does not require forfeiting your own vision of who you are. Stand up for your own outlook on life with quiet confidence. You will command the respect of others in doing so.

When you turn to the Christian community for a clear and unified voice, here again you find such a wide range of conflicting testimonies about what Jesus Christ is and what he should mean to you that you are tempted to sit on the fence and watch those testimonies go by. The cults form around your spiritual concern like mushrooms overnight. Each has a demanding, coercing pseudo-certainty that tweaks your skepticism. This is a far cry from the prayer of Jesus that his disciples may be one as he and God in heaven are one. Even in the face of these persuasive diversities, though, I appeal to you to choose what you believe and whom you will serve.

Waiting for a "Lucky Break"

Another force within you keeps you on the fence of indecision—the fond hope that a "lucky break" will do away with all your frustration, that all your desires will be fulfilled by chance. In the meantime, you hold your life in suspense, waiting until your break comes. You cloak your lack of confidence in this way.

Daniel Yankelovich says (p. 236), "The Christian injunction that to find oneself one must first lose oneself contains an essential truth any seeker of self-fulfillment needs to grasp." Such an injunction pulls you off the fence. You cease to dream of a lucky meeting of your star with that star of a "big break" that will drop complete self-fulfillment in your lap.

A Wounded Capacity for Commitment

If you are the dreamer I just described, you have every right to feel that my description gives you a hard time, even hassles you a bit. Before you turn me off, though, let me say that an underlying cause of your procrastination, dreaming, and indecision may well be a wounded capacity for commitment. Early in your life, you may have been handed from one person to another, not one of whom really invested much time, energy, or devotion in you. About the time you became attached to one person and place, you were moved, handed off to someone else. If you have any memory of these wounds to your efforts to attach yourself to someone significant, you may remember protesting loudly when you were taken away from the person to whom you were attached. Then you fell into despair. The despair hurt so badly that you ceased to care in order to protect yourself. You just did not recommit yourself to anyone or anything for fear of being hurt again.

Later on in life, you may have ventured out to give yourself to a religious group. Then something bad happened in the group, and once again you protested and fell into despair. It hurt so badly again that you ceased to care. That is one way of stopping the pain. Now, when it comes to committing yourself to a set of convictions that give you confidence, you prefer to sit on the fence and watch from a distance rather than get involved again. Commitments make you a target for getting hurt; at least that's the way you feel, that is your perception. But having convictions that give you confidence implies that the beliefs and persons in which and in whom you have invested confidence are trustworthy. There is a steadfastness and reliability about them. They can be counted on.

The real question is, "Can wounded capacities to commit yourself be healed?" Of course, scars will always be there, but yes, they can be healed through daring to be hurt again. You can use the knowledge gained through having been hurt before to understand your own childlike naiveté. You become, as Jesus said, "wise as serpents and innocent as doves." This is the value of learning by experience rather than letting painful experiences disenchant you with life as a whole. The psalmist said, "I said, in my consternation, 'Men are all a vain hope.' " Now *some* persons *are* a vain hope. *Some* persons *will* let you down. However, do not let your painfully formed conviction that *no one* is trustworthy keep you on the fence of indecision. Such a hastily formed conviction, born out of anger and consternation, does you harm; it undermines your own self-confidence.

Not Enough Information

If you are to have convictions that give you confidence, you must set out to discover for yourself who and what can and cannot be trusted. You lack information about organizations and persons. You have not yet had face-to-face "hands on" dealings with them. You have not put them to the test, or yourself in relation to them. Many of your information is hearsay, secondhand. Some of your information is not fact but error. Many of your thoughts are simply blank—*no* information. You know a lot of things that firsthand investigation will prove to be false. Some of it will be true. Much of it will be *news* to you! As F. H. Giddings, one of the pioneers in American sociology, says, in "The Scientific Scrutiny of Societal Facts," "I want to believe it; but then, *is it* always or generally [so]? Does anybody *know* that it usually is, or is everybody just *saying* that it is?" (see V. F. Calverton, ed., *The Making of Society,* p. 612). This spirit of skeptical inquiry starts you on your own fact-finding expedition as you come down off the fence. You begin to find your own personal stance toward life. This stance becomes the bulwark of your own confidence—in your own eyes, in the eyes of your neighbors, and in the eyes of God.

A thirty-year-old man told me of his having shucked off the external and formal religious beliefs of his parents when he was sixteen. At eighteen, he was drafted into the army, although he is a conscientious objector. Neither his home pastor nor a neighbor on the draft board would support him in his application for conscientious objector status, so—he was drafted. While in the army he became a part of a "Jesus group" that memorized Scriptures and prayed together. This meant a lot to him for a while, but then he found their ready-made answers too easy to cover the large doubts he held. From then until I met him, about ten years later, he had no confidence in his own judgment or in what he had been taught. Now, however, he has come down off the fence of indecision and started a persistent search for personally chosen beliefs that he can live by and be an example to his children. This search began, remarkably enough, as he and his wife anticipated the birth of their son. This was a time of seeking out, a teachable moment. But whatever he chooses must be *his* choice, not mine or anyone else's for him.

This spirit of inquiry was what prompted Luke, the beloved physician, to go "over the whole course of events" in the life of Jesus "in detail" for himself. He wanted to give his readers "authentic knowledge," as the New English Bible puts it, so that his readers might "know the truth," as the Revised Standard Version puts it, or, in the words of the King James Version, "That you mightest know the certainty of those things, wherein thou hast been instructed." Knowing the truth to be authentic knowledge and arriving conclusively at its certainty takes searching, researching, and testing of evidence on your part. As you come down off the fence, you have made a decision that having convictions that give you confidence is no spectator sport. You must get into the thick of the action yourself. As you begin to examine firsthand the documents of your own spiritual history and compare them with the meaty content of the New Testament and its contenders for your loyalty, you gather confidence as you go. You have eyes; use them. You have ears; use them. You have good intelligence; use it. Confidence in your eyes, ears, intelligence, and judgment comes to you as it does to your muscles: through exercising them.

On Your Way to Certainty

The alternative to the futility of indecision and fence-sitting is to choose some clear-cut agreement about your own principles that gives you confidence and sets you on your way to productive living. This does not happen by just jumping down and saying to yourself, "I am on my way." To the contrary, some specific disciplines await you.

You need to learn some things to give substance to your certainties. You need some specific starting and continuing points of reference, much as an airline pilot does who arrives at a destination by having periodic radio checkpoints along the way.

This calls for carefully collecting data about your history from friends and relatives. It calls for consulting with professionals you respect about your basic abilities and how to fit your past work, study, and worship life into an adult design that will be best for you. This fact-finding may also include a survey of what places exist where you can work, study, and make a living. It may involve intense conversation with your spouse, if you are married, and with your children, if they are old enough to talk with you. You need a spiritual director to guide you in this search. Seek out a person whom you already respect.

Check Out Your Heritage Now

Before you become airborne on your way to certainty, you need to run a thorough check of all the vital parts of your life that have brought you this far. Check out both the contradictions and the unique genius of your heritage. Both are there. You are a part of all you have met. Your lack of confidence *and* your sense of strength may well come from messages from your past that keep inserting themselves again and again into your thinking about yourself in relation to others. You may have had teachings drilled into you that you really did not believe or trust from the start. Yet people you needed badly at the time and probably loved in your own way said that this was what you were to believe. In order to keep the peace and stay in their good graces, you assented to the teaching. You may also have had people who believed in you when you did not believe in yourself. They braced you up when you were discouraged, calmed you when you were afraid, and opened doors of opportunity for you that you could not open for yourself. If so, who were they? Now you are free to reject some of their teachings and accept others. What positive replacements come along now for what you have rejected? You have been intimidated by the negative and have not had the self-assurance to make up your own mind. Decide now to draw on the positive strengths.

Daniel Yankelovich makes a distinction between liberation and freedom. Liberation is concerned with your *right* to think your own thoughts, with restoring rights that have been lost or abused. Freedom, however, is what you *do* with your liberation. What you do determines whether or not you are free. We are called to put all the convictions of our forebears to the test; if they are true, we are to make them our own. If they are not, we are to find what *is* true.

The example of Alex Haley, the author of the book *Roots,* is helpful. Through education, hard work, and much providential care, he had struck off some of the shackles of a segregated people. He set about reexamining and reassessing his heritage. Was it all bad? Was there anything good that came out of Africa in the slave trade? He chose to retrace the journey of a slave ship to America and live under the conditions—as nearly as possible—that the slaves did. The journey thrust him into a depression that made him contemplate suicide. As he stood on the deck of the ship thinking of casting himself overboard, he suddenly became aware of the remarkable wisdom, strength, and courage of his people. Their voices seemed to be saying, "Tell our story for us." It was then he grasped the power and productivity of his African forebears. He laid hold of the strengths of his heritage.

My point is this: Everybody's heritage, no matter how unacceptable to us now, has some strengths for productive living that provide a powerhouse of convictions that give us confidence. Yet we do not gain access to this strength until we consciously and intentionally reassess our heritage. This calls for getting past the negatives of our parents and hometown and laying our hands lovingly upon the strengths of personhood they gave us. I want you to do this much earlier in your life than I did in mine. Don't wait; start now. One way to do this is to "reconnect" with parents, brothers, sisters, aunts, uncles, and cousins and reconstruct an oral history of your family. Shake fact from fancy; make note of stories and legends; look past the noisy dogmatists to the quiet people who gave you wisdom, comfort, and self-reliance. Decide what you are thankful for in your heritage. Affirm it now. As you do this, you are on your way, bringing the ark of the covenant of your family with you and laying aside the weights and sins bequeathed to you.

Decide What You Don't Believe

Your protests are a part of your convictions. Standing up for what you *don't* believe immediately gets you off your seat on the fence of indecision. Therefore, decide clearly what you do *not* believe. This is a peeling-away process. To put away a belief, however, calls for the same testing process as does adopting a positive belief. Copernicus doubted that the world was flat and opened a whole new era of science. The severe testing of medieval Catholic beliefs about the confessional, about praying for the dead, and about priests taking money and selling indulgences was an agonizing process for Martin Luther. Lech Walesa in Poland doubts the dogmas of communism and gives his Nobel Peace Prize money to others.

Yet you, like many others, may have been required since childhood, to get in line with other people's persuasions. You may feel shame, guilt, or even sin before God if you doubt these convictions of others. For you, to doubt is to be an outcast. But doubt is not the opposite of faith. Honest doubt is the beginning of discovery and adventure into new worlds of truth. Honest doubt can be the seedbed for growing your own convictions that will give you confidence for the living of these days. As Tennyson said in "In Memoriam":

> There lives more faith in honest doubt,
> Believe me, than in all the creeds.

But don't let doubt become a way of life, in which you

dodge the responsibility of collecting information, weighing evidence, and forming convictions based on your own experience. Tennyson describes *honest* doubt, not doubt as a smoke screen. Be willing to search your history and inner self and the world around you for those unshakable commitments that make your old shaky insecurity unnecessary. Arriving at solid conclusions as to what you honestly do *not* believe clears the air for you to see what you *do* believe. At the risk of rejection by others, you can say, "Here I stand!"

Where Won't You Bend?

As you shed the externals, the convictions of other people that you cannot affirm, you also come across beliefs that these same others have shared with you which common sense and your genuine love for them enable you to confess have given you the framework that has brought you safely this far. You embrace as your own, therefore, the genius of your informal and formal teachers. You refuse to reject *everything* you have been taught. Even if you have a deep running hostility toward parents, teachers, and pastors of your past, admit that at this point and that point you are indeed a part of all those you have met. A clock that won't run is still right twice a day. Don't argue with it at those precise moments!

When I say heritage and refer to "all those you have met," I mean far more than merely your immediate family. I mean the group of friends (and enemies!) with whom you grew up, your ethnic group as it relates to other ethnic communities, your educational pilgrimage from one school to another, and the imprints of pride, prejudice, and deep-running convictions these people and events have made upon you as a person. These imprints either cut you off from or give you access to a security and confidence in what you believe. You may be ashamed of your connections with these persons and groups. Reexamine that sense of shame. You may find that it obscures the genuine power of personhood you have to offer to the world. To see this is another of many moments of truth for you.

Yes, those particular moments of truth stuck. They gave you the backbone to face rather than run from life. Think of your backbone literally. Your spine is a marvel of engineering wisdom. It supports your whole frame. By bending in complex patterns of motion, it enables you to do hundreds of tasks. Yet there are points beyond which it will not bend. If it would bend beyond these limits, your life itself would be in danger. If it were totally rigid and would not bend at all, life would, to say the least, be miserable and you could not function. Convictions that give you confidence are like that. Those that are central to your integrity are flexible, but they have limits beyond which they will not bend or compromise.

Ask yourself what the issues in your life are about which you will not bend versus those about which you are quite flexible. What are the "unbendables" and what are the peripheral beliefs in your life? What do you put at the spotlight of your attention and what is at the outer dark circumference of your awareness? Does this give you confidence or frighten you?

Steadfastness in Holding to Your Priorities

Earlier I referred to our capacity for commitment. Being committed wholeheartedly and without mental reservations is the stuff of which confidence is made. Your commitment of your intelligence, your attention, your time, your energy, and your money to implementing a personal persuasion is the wellspring of your personal certainty. The prophet Elijah, in challenging his people about their worship of idols rather than the Lord God, said, "How long will you go limping with two different opinions?" (1 Kings 18:21). Jesus said, "No one can serve two masters; for either he [or she] will hate the one and love the other, or . . . will be devoted to one and despise the other" (Matt. 6:24). When Jesus also said, "Blessed are the pure in heart, for they shall see God" (Matt. 5:8), he set the tone for the whole teaching of the Sermon on the Mount. You and I cannot spend our energies pursuing material security, hating our enemies, living a life controlled entirely by sex, hunger, and ambition—and love God at the same time. These become our gods.

To be single-heartedly devoted to God is purity of heart. Purity of heart is not a goody-two-shoes, spick-and-span freedom of several minor moral offenses. Purity of heart is wholehearted commitment to God. Limping between this devotion and devotion to lesser realities gives you "double vision"; you cannot see God. The Letter of James calls it being "a double-minded person, unstable in all our ways" (James 1:8). Therein lies the lack of confidence you and I experience. We are not sure of our own point of view. Therefore, getting "on your way" with a calm and steady assurance of your personal integrity before God calls for an agonizing appraisal in your own particular wilderness of choice.

Keeping Flexible

The purpose of the following chapters is to provide several time-tested, biblically and theologically serious, and psychologically demonstrable guidelines for arriving at your own convictions that will give you confidence. Such foundations of your faith necessarily must be developed in such a way that they will flex with the changes and shocks of the years unfolding ahead. They will need to have growing room that will enable you to "graduate" from one era of your life and commence another without being torn apart. These convictions will need to be strong enough and ethically sound enough to give you a reasonable degree of security in the right and wrong choices you make in a world of amoral confusion. Furthermore, these certainties will need to be comprehensive enough to enable you to relate with understanding to people who come from circumstances different from your own and have ways of life that give them courage to live productively in those circumstances. In other words, your conclusions about life must be such that you are not shocked but stirred to learn when you are challenged by a person of a background, culture, race, religion, or ethical outlook different from your own.

This last specification of the kinds of convictions that will sustain your confidence implies another facet to the jewel of your belief system: Whatever the stage of your maturity, you need to be *open* enough to let in new light from new discoveries. When solid new evidence comes to you, the staunchest conclusion can be reevaluated. In this sense you become a lifelong seeker after more wisdom. You confess at all times that you know in part and pray that you may understand fully, as the apostle Paul does in 1 Corinthians 13:12. Yet he could also say, "I know whom I have believed, and I am sure that he is able to guard until that Day what has been entrusted to me" (2 Tim. 1:12).

Finally, you notice that the apostle Paul does *not* say, "I know *what* I believe," he says, "I know *whom* I believe." Convictions center down to *persons,* not abstract, foggy creeds, statements of principles, or philosophical dogmas. Choosing a leader you can trust without being betrayed, follow without fear of being misled, rely upon without being let down has a way of putting flesh and blood on your convictions. Often I talk with persons who feel that God has betrayed them, misled them, and let them down in the crunch of human suffering. They say things about God I would wholeheartedly agree with—if I believed in a god like the one they believe in. But when they join me in contrasting what they believe about God with what Jesus *did* in the days of his flesh, it just does not add up. For example, "Why did God kill my baby?" I find Jesus as a baby whom Herod tried, without success, to slaughter, but I do not find Jesus killing babies. Neither does God kill babies.

Therefore, consider your convictions in the light of *who* it is that captures your wholehearted commitment. Hear me out both here and throughout the following pages. I unashamedly point you to Jesus of Nazareth, who is the Christ, as that Person on whom you can trust, whom you can choose as a leader, and upon whom you can rely without being let down.

The Power of Faith in Adversity

You do not come to a time of shaken confidence in your own convictions without having been overwhelmed by adversity. You may have had many cherished devotions in life. Yet you have been disillusioned, let down, and even betrayed by others as you have tried to practice these commitments. You may have seen others sail along with the full wind of success seemingly behind them, pushing them ahead. You, however, have had your hopes turned to ashes as one great reversal is hardly over before you face another.

Yet these afflictions are time-bound. They run their course. As the apostle Paul says, they are "but for the moment." Hidden within them is a kind of learning, a revelation of God's own steadfast character, waiting for your closer inspection. Your faith in the Eternal puts things that run their course, that are "but for the moment," in a larger perspective. The active Spirit of the living God does with you as with Paul as he faced Ananias in the council of priests' trial of him: "The following night the Lord stood by him and said, 'Take courage, for as you have testified about me at Jerusalem, so you must bear witness also at Rome' " (Acts 23:11). God stands by you. You are inspired to take courage.

In this story, Paul had just engaged in a fiery debate over principles and beliefs about the resurrection. The Pharisees and Sadducees got into a "great clamor" with each other. It became a hot academic debate between opposing sides. Much heat and no light came out of it. That is what can happen when principles and persons are torn apart from each other. Convictions become powerful in time of adversity when they are embodied, incarnated, and become a living relationship between persons who care for each other, stand by each other through thick and thin, and give courage to each other when otherwise they would be engulfed in loneliness. This gives assurance of things hoped for and the conviction of things not seen. When the clamor of the debate was over and Paul was alone at night, the resurrected Lord was not a belief to clamor about; he was a Presence from whom Paul drew companionship and courage.

Therefore, having the courage of your convictions is not a task you perform alone, screwing up your own courage and blustering with a false sense of bravado. No, the Lord stands by you, and this Lord is one who has been through the fiery trials by ordeal, through death, beyond the gates of hell, and been resurrected. You participate in that resurrection with him by your faith in his Presence as he stands by you. If you were childlike enough to ask, "Lord, how did you get here to tell me to take courage and to stand by me?", then you would have a long story of adversities through which his faith brought him. He endured the cross. He conquered death. Now, nothing can separate you from him, "neither death, nor life, nor angels, nor principalities, nor things present, nor things to come, nor powers, nor height, nor depth, nor anything else in all creation" (Rom. 8:38–39).

Your loneliness is met and driven away by the strength of his Presence. At the core of our being, we are not alone when we invest our faith in the One who stands by us and gives us courage and comradeship through adversity.

Chapter 2

Working Out Convictions in Your Own Wilderness

You may have inherited a great many beliefs to which you have given lip service in order to reverence your parents and grandparents. They are curios in museum cases in your mind. They are not tools of competence for you in the grimier tasks you have to do every day. Or you may have collected them the way a huge snowball collects things as it is pushed along in the snow by a crowd of playmates. You are glad to have other people to "tour" your beliefs and very willing to be a "tour guide." When it comes to giving you a sense of certainty when all else around you is being shaken, though, these beliefs are too flimsy to be of use. They hardly merit the name conviction because in no way are you persuaded or convinced of their truth *for you.*

Let me give you an example. John Bunyan lived from 1628 to 1688 near Bedford, England. He was a tinker, a traveling mender of pots, pans, kettles, and so on. He was largely self-educated, after having learned to read and write in school. When he was sixteen both his mother and his sister died within a month of each other, his father married again, and he himself was drafted into Cromwell's army because civil war had just broken out. He saw little actual fighting, but this became his own personal wilderness of the spirit. He was caught up in the seething religious life of Cromwell's army. Preaching captains, Quakers, Seekers, Ranters were questioning all authority of the established church except that of individual conscience. Bunyan was stirred deeply by this and began to read the newly translated King James Version of the Bible. Upon discharge from the army in July 1647, he continued to wrestle and labor in agonizing temptations, sieges of despair. However, he moved through the course of grim struggle and the teachings of Calvin about the predestination of a person in terms of his own real needs and the evidence of growth in his convictions to a spiritual integrity of his own before God.

He emerged from his wilderness to write and preach with powerful persuasiveness. He said, "I went myself in Chains to speak to them in Chains, and carried that Fire in my own conscience that I persuaded them to beware of." Out of this encounter in his own personal wilderness, John Bunyan wrote his enduring allegory of the spiritual pilgrimage of the self, *The Pilgrim's Progress*. Here he tells the story of his journey from the City of Destruction to the Celestial City, his sure dwelling place in God's love. He falls into pits of despond, has to do battle with opponents all along the way, and meets people who trick, mislead, and ridicule him. He forms friendships with people who let him down and do all manner of ill against him. Along the way, though, he also meets greathearted, faithful, and dependable interpreters of the way he must go. In short, the imaginative journey was a gripping and shocking shift from agony to ecstasy and back again. Nothing came easy. He experienced the journey himself and lived through it.

This story, next to the Bible, is one of the most widely read in the English language. Nathaniel Hawthorne, the American novelist who lived from 1804 to 1864, read it and contrasted it with the religious convictions of people of his day in a satire called "The Celestial Railroad." Two hundred years after *The Pilgrim's Progress*, Hawthorne dreams that he visits Bunyan's City of Destruction. He discovers that a businessman, Mr. Smooth-It-Away, though he himself has never visited the Celestial City, has all sorts of facts *about* the City. He and some of his townsmen have built a railroad from the City of Destruction to the Celestial City. They organize *tours* that take people in the smooth comfort of a railroad car, with all their burdens packed in a separate baggage car. By paying a sum of money, people can observe from a distance all the places Bunyan's Christian traveled. And they can do this without any inconvenience, struggle, agony, or ecstasy. They just watch! The punch line of the story comes at the *end* of the train ride. The train stops short of the Celestial City, and no one has any more confidence that they will be able to enter than if they had never taken the tourists' journey.

These stories converge on one conclusion: You will not come to convictions of your own by the spectator sport of watching others work as they hammer out their beliefs on the anvil of personal experience. Being a tourist relieves you of the responsibility of taking your stand as a working citizen of a territory of truth. To shape and fashion our own personal convictions, you and I must make our own pilgrimage, be led into our own wilderness to an agonizing reappraisal of what we have always believed, to a face-to-face set of choices about the kind of person we are and what we are going to become.

So, then, join me in ruling out the halfhearted tourist approach that gawks, looks, takes pictures, gets bored, and looks for some new thing. We are not going to be souvenir collectors of this conversation piece of conviction or of that jewel we found in a distant country and display them in order to amuse our guests. No, what we bring back from our own wilderness may well be too deep for words, but nevertheless the convictions we hold are translated regularly into behaviors as we move confidently among confused people in a chaotic world.

What Is Your Wilderness?

I have used the metaphor of a wilderness from the experience of Jesus described in Mark 1:12–13, Matthew 4:1–11, and Luke 4:1–13. Earlier, Moses had spent years in a wilderness, when he ran from Egypt after killing an Egyptian. And Paul spent silent years in Arabia after having defected from the Jewish hierarchy and joined the Christian people of the Way.

You may have read these familiar stories often. For you, the picture of a "wilderness" is a faraway, unimaginable one. Let me try to make it more personal. Do not think of the wilderness of your life as a desert in Palestine. Think of your own inner world as a yet unexplored and uncharted region of your very self. Think of yourself as "wandering" without a clear sense of inner direction. Now picture yourself as having a private inner world all your own and as getting "lost" in your own thoughts. These thoughts are turning over choices and decisions, and the feelings you have about those choices and decisions. These thoughts are so busy that if you awaken at night they take over, and rather than sleep you move rapidly from one to the other. If you do sleep, you may dream about them. You are trying to work out *what* you think, *what* you are going to do, and *why* you think and do what you decide. This is your wilderness, when decision time is at hand and you are struggling in the inmost parts of your being to choose what you stand for and what you are going to do about it. These choices take outward form, and yet the outward, surface realities of your life have an inward depth, a spiritual territory in which you assign them meaning and direction.

What is your particular wilderness? Let me suggest a few possibilities of the outward forms your personal wilderness may take. Try these thoughts on for their possible fit. See how they connect with that inner realm of decision-making and choices I have just described.

An Impossible Work Situation

Your work situation may be your wilderness. You may be a "housewife," not employed outside the home. Earlier your children were small preschoolers and demanded all your time. Now the youngest is in elementary school. You have about four hours a day in which you would like to do something creative, challenging, and exciting. You get restless. You even fret. You cast about. You dream about what you would like to be, become, and do. If you are a mother whose children are grown and out of the house, the issues are more intense. What new kinds of decisions need to be made to make the most of the rest of your life? As you struggle in this wilderness, what temptations beset you and what challenges to courageous commitment do you face?

Then again, whether you are male or female, the chances are high that you are employed on a job or struggling to find one. I hear people refer to the place they work as a "jungle," as "chaos," as a "desert," and many such terms. People without work say, "I don't want just *any* job." Many people in their jobs move from one conflict situation to another. They are pressured and tested again and again to think, say, do, and be things they do not believe in or want to be. They are expected to make bricks without straw, turn stones into bread, and walk on water to accomplish goals other people, not they, have chosen. They live out their lives in pale terror and quiet desperation. They yearn for deliverance. Yet they are too accustomed to their bonds of security to rise up and cast them off. They are too locked into one alternative for existence—namely, this job—to take a leap of faith toward any other alternative.

Yet they do not want to go to work in the morning. When they return in the evening, they spend the dinner hour and the evening rehashing hurts and indignities—perceived or actual—that have been heaped upon them. They become exhausted from the stress, their perception becomes distorted, and they are tempted to do some very rash and stupid things. This impossible job is their particular wilderness. You are no tourist here!

Loneliness

You may find yourself living alone in a large city. It is difficult for you to meet new friends, much less develop close friendships. You may enjoy your school or your work, but your associates do not socialize with each other often. All sorts of "purchased friendships" are available, but you do not have enough money to join groups, go on excursions, cruises, and many other things that push people into the instant intimacies that happen on one-hour *Love Boats*.

Therefore, you spend a lot of time by yourself and are forced by this loneliness in a crowd to look inward at your own feelings. Long walks to museums, art galleries, concerts—alone—give you opportunity to face up to yourself and be tested as to what you really believe, to see whence comes your confidence to face life rather than to run home.

This is your wilderness, and you are being tested.

Earlier I spoke of our needing convictions to hold us steady when everything around us is being shaken. You may never have felt all else around you being shaken. Yet if you have just entered the military—be it as sailor, soldier, airperson, or marine—you are being tested at every point as to what you stand for. And what you stand for is itself being stressed at the very points of your day-to-day behavior. This tour of duty is no tourist's sight-seeing jaunt. The method of training is a hands-on kind. The luxury of flunking out is not a ready option. You perform whether you choose to do so or not. How do you maintain your own individuality under such regimentation? People from all stations of life are around you questioning, teasing, making fun, and seeing if you are "real" and "can take it."

This may be your wilderness, your time of testing to make or break you. If you have already been in the service and possibly are a combat veteran, your memories of that time may be such that you want to reassess what convictions were formed during your hitch in the service. What quiet resolves did you make then? How are those resolves supplying you with confidence for living now? This may be or may have been your wilderness, your time of arriving at those convictions that steady you, give you courage, and inspire you with hope.

Unsatisfactory Relationships

Another crucial situation can become a wilderness of self-examination and agonizing choices for many people. That situation is to have an overwhelming desire frustrated, denied, and shut off completely in a deeply personal relationship. It just won't come right.

Obviously, the most intense expressions of such relationships are in a person's love life, especially within the boundaries of marriage. A partner is repetitively unfaithful, but with most of your life already invested in the marriage, do you just grin and bear it and act as if nothing is wrong? Or your mate is so preoccupied with work, community activities, or even church life that every evening you are left alone to your own thoughts, wishes, hopes, and frustrations. Attempts to communicate are few because opportunity for them appears so rarely. You die lonely indeed, and this is your wilderness.

Or take the frustrated hope to have children. I have agonized with young people who as married couples yearn to have a child and, in spite of all their efforts and medical expense, remain childless. The young wife mourns her childlessness and fights the battle between a sometimes meaningless job to help pay the household bills and the unfulfilled longing to be a mother caring for her baby. The pain is heightened when she sees and hears of couples who have children they do not want or welcome. That pain becomes acute when she hears of a woman who has an abortion. The spiritual straits of this wilderness become a testing ground for her and her husband. To arrive at a sustaining set conviction about life that will hold them and their marriage together over the long pull of the years ahead becomes their struggle of the spirit.

Also, I have seen single persons who suffer severe rejection by a prospective mate whom they love with an undying devotion. One of my teachers, Anton Boisen, lived to be ninety-one years of age. In his youth he fell in love with Alice Batchelder, who cared for him as a friend and as a person but rejected his proposals of marriage. Boisen lived out his years as a single person. He says (p. 2) of his agony over not finding favor with the woman he loved:

> There came a love affair which swept me off my feet. . . . On her part it was a source of great embarrassment, but she gave me a helping hand at the critical moment and stood ready to undertake what for her was a task of mercy. But I failed to make the grade.

His failure was the triggering factor in a serious emotional breakdown, which was the "critical moment" of which he speaks. He describes his illness as "the little known wilderness of the inner life" (p. 12). He chose to explore this wilderness with an "ever-deepening conviction" that his purpose in life was to understand and treat other emotionally disturbed persons and to teach others to do so also. He recovered to make a lasting contribution to the education of ministers, of whom I had the privilege of being one.

Indoctrination

Your unique wilderness of struggle for your deepened convictions may be different from any I have mentioned. However, your experience calls you out of a mere inheritance of or lip service to this or that idea about life. You arrive at a deepened conviction that provides you with a clear sense of direction for living. You develop a profound resolve that gives you motivation and courage to put newly discovered convictions into action.

One hazard you face in your inner struggle for personally chosen convictions is that pat answers will be pushed on you by others that may not be right for you. You will do better by moving further into your own personal wilderness, until you connect up with what really is right for you, than by being indoctrinated by a sacred or secular propagandist, whether Christian or Jewish, positivist or Marxist. Avoid what Theodore Roszak experienced (p. 385):

> I vividly recall my own mind-murdering struggles with the Catholic catechism in childhood. Question and answer, question and answer . . . a jackbooted parade of lifeless verbal formulas, every one of them to be recited letter perfect, every one of them to be literally believed under threat of corporal punishment. Dogma and doctrine were marched through my brain like storm troops flattening every natural barrier childish inquisitiveness might raise. It was open warfare on young imagination.

I covenant with you that even though in this book I appeal directly to the experience of Jesus of Nazareth and the God whom he worshiped, I will respect and cherish your right to a supreme vision of your own. My concern is that you be on your own before God in the struggle in your own wilderness. I have confidence in both you and God as to the shape your convictions take. *My* certainties, at best, can give you only momentary security. *Your* certainties, put into action, will go with you throughout life. Therefore, in our conversation together, I will hold out to the end for your own inner persuasions instead of mine. They are between you and God. I will pose issues for your reflection. You will dispose of them on your own before God.

Hazards in Working Out Convictions

Whatever your wilderness may be and whatever specific commitments you make as a result, I can say with confidence that all enduring convictions in human life are formed successfully in spite of very common hazards. These hazards were met by Jesus during his temptation in the wilderness, and his example shows us how to persevere in working out our own values.

Inescapable Bewilderments of Being Human

You are bewildered as to what direction to take when you come to a crossroad in your life's path. You are confused and cannot see your way through the tangle of competing demands on your very human self. Some of these bewilderments arise from our simply being human. They come with the territory.

Jesus of Nazareth was human in the days of his flesh. He was subjected to all the limitations and bewilderments of being human that you and I are. Believing that Jesus was human has been disputed throughout Christian history. To believe that Jesus was completely human in the years of his earthly life is harder for conventional Christians to accept than to believe that he is divine. I have already noted the dramatic accounts of his entering his own personal wilderness to work out the bewildering choices inherent in his being human, just as you and I. Often these accounts are described as the "temptations in the wilderness" or "the tests in the wilderness." Sometimes they are called "the decisions in the wilderness" or "the choices in the wilderness." However we name them, these experiences of Jesus seem to me to be universal tests, decisions, or choices that require all persons to deny or affirm their own basic humanness. To accept our humanness gives a life of confidence in the face of adversity, threat, and frustration. To deny our humanness sets us up for a life of insecurity, fear, and fretful anxiety.

The story in the New Testament is a powerful drama of

the contention between the Spirit of God and the spirit of Satan, the god of deception, chaos, destruction, and evil. We miss the point today in our feeble attempts at recognizing that evil is present, organized, and active in the world and in our lives. We do so by denying that evil becomes *personified* just as goodness does. The devil is no horned and forked-tailed creature here, there, or yonder, such as I used to see pictured on cans of Red Devil lye. The devil is the personification of one's self-deception and worship of idols. Before it can operate, you and I must cooperate in the lies, the self-deception, and the idolatry. It is a spiritual transaction of human choice, not a bodily presence, except as we, like Peter, provide the bodily presence in our cooperation. Led by the Spirit of God, Jesus arrived at working answers to the question of how he would live his life with courage, strength, and self-control. The issues he decided to be crucial were the rejection of the self-serving magic and the affirmation of the long-range satisfactions of the life of the spirit, the rejection of the self-centered uses of power and the consecration of power to the worship of God, and the rejection of the temptation to consider himself an exception to the basic laws of the universe in behalf of working with God in harmony with the creation.

Self-serving Magic in the Face of Frustration

Jesus was hungry, for he had eaten nothing for forty days. "The devil said to him, 'If you are the Son of God, command this stone to become bread' " (Luke 4:3). "Bread" stands for any gratification of wants: hunger, thirst, sexual desire, compulsion to work, money. For Jesus on that day it was bread. In the sum of things, we live by the word of God, he said.

Turning stones into bread when you are hungry—what a test of a frustrated person! Human fantasy takes over when a basic hunger, as for food, sex, or economic security, is both intense and frustrated. We would welcome a short, quick fix. Magic would do that! Magic is the art or group of arts that *pretends* to be able to compel any unknown force, God, or any supernatural power to obey the wishes of the magician. The Mediterranean world of Jesus' day was full of fakers, masters at pretense, as is the whole world of today. Jesus had to choose whether he was going to be a faker or whether he was going to be for real. Satan was later described by Jesus as the "father of lies," the great pretender, who appealed to Jesus to be a short-cut magician. Jesus replied, "It is written, 'Man shall not live by bread alone' " (Luke 4:4).

In reality, there are no shortcuts to genuine satisfaction. Yet the faker pretends that there are, pretends that you and I can create an imaginary world of our own which resolves all our frustrated appetites instantly. Good judgment tells us this is not so, but we would prefer to believe it is true. Therefore, as one unknown humorist puts it:

> We sit in a green grotto
> With a bucket of lurid paint
> And paint the thing that isn't
> For the great god of things as they ain't!

Think, if you will, of the person who lives in a dream-world assuming that, without the drudgery of learning, discipline, and hard work, a big break will come along. He or she will be on easy street. This is what Dan Kiley calls "the Peter Pan Syndrome" in men and what Colette Dowling calls "the Cinderella Complex" in women. The man does not *do* the apprentice work to become a master craftsman, musician, or thinker. Learning tools and their uses, notes and scales in music, or the languages in which thoughts are expressed is beneath him. By wishing, he thinks these things will simply *be*. Or, because he assumes he is special, they will be his for the asking, and not the result of years of tedious discipline. Magic will work *for* him, he thinks, because he is a selected, chosen person! Peter Pan was all those things in his own mind.

Or the woman assumes that her Prince Charming will come along and deliver her from the situation she is in. She will be taken care of by a magical godmother who causes all these things to happen. The tedium of learning skills, developing competency, and becoming an authentic person in her own right are the long route for her. She prefers to imagine that someday she will be magically taken care of without effort on her part.

What a set of beliefs! What grand assumptions! They certainly obscure our basic humanness and keep us oblivious to the realities of working it out in our own wilderness. Yet underneath our naive assumptions we are uneasy, uncertain, afraid to have our mettle tested, and filled with the fear of failure. If we prefer the imaginary security of magical thinking to the risk of putting our fantasies away so we can live in the real world, we become fakers. That is the choice we make.

Yet you and I are not shut up to the fate of being fakers. At the risk of going hungry for a few days or weeks, at the risk of trying and not succeeding the first hundred times, at the risk of having other fakers chide and make sport of us, we take the longer route of acceptance as one of the human race. We take the hard course of personal discipline rather than the deceptive route of magic. In the long run, being a faker *is* the destructive route. Satan is not only the father of lies, as Jesus says, but also the Destroyer, as Paul says in 1

Corinthians 10:10. The choice, then, is not between a safe route and a risky one. The choice is between a route that is creative in the long run and one that is destructive in the long run. The *false* sense of safety is in the shortcut perspective. The *true* sense of security is in the long-run perception. Psychoanalysts today speak of this in a secular manner. They speak of a person renouncing the *pleasure principle* of immediate satisfaction for the *reality principle* of more enduring satisfaction.

In the struggle in your own personal wilderness, then, you choose between being the faker-magician or the genuinely human person. You and I are always being tested—and testing ourselves—as to whether we are for real. The crux of the test is in the way we handle the pressure of an immediate hunger's being frustrated, as Jesus did. Stephen Neill says (p. 206), "No man in history can ever have been hemmed in by the realities of frustration than did Jesus of Nazareth. . . . It is deeply moving to see what Jesus makes of all this." In his wilderness, struggling with his own humanity, Jesus reveals our true selves to you and me as we struggle with our many hungers in our own wilderness.

A Devilish Pact for Power

In a flash, the devil showed Jesus all the kingdoms of the world. Then he offered him a deal, a pact. "I can give the power of all these kingdoms and the glory that goes with it to anyone I choose. If you will do homage to me, it will be yours." His offer demanded complete allegiance in return. That was the deal. Those were the strings attached to the offer of total power. The sneaky deception lay in Satan's comment that the power of all the kingdoms of the world had been put in his hands. When someone falls for this fiction, he or she *becomes* the incarnation of evil. Satan must take the form of human beings as individuals and as groups. Satan is a *counterfeit* messiah who thrives on our lust for power and our capacity for self-deception. We are snared by the desire to be a god. I suppose the plainest everyday experience of this is when you and I are flattered and fawned over by other people. We are both uncomfortable and enchanted when this happens. Watch the enchantment and follow the discomfort. Then laugh at yourself! Shakespeare pinpoints the subtlety of flattery in *Julius Caesar:*

> But when I tell him he hates flatterers,
> He says he does, being then most flattered.

On this wisdom, then, it is better to refuse to take flatterers seriously than to hate them.

But Jesus did not do this. He said, "You shall worship the Lord your God and him only shall you serve" (Matt. 4:10). He refused to be the dwelling place for the devil, the homing device of the lust for absolute power. This pact can be and is offered to each individual, group, or nation. Whether your struggle is a pitched battle for power with your classmates at school, with your parents at home, with your spouse in a marital conflict, between your union and management, with your competitors for a promotion, or with your children who are in rebellion against you, the need to be in total control is the beguiling opportunity for self-deception. The name of these games is the struggle for power.

Do not think I am saying no to *all* exercises of human power. Far from it. Your sense of competence to do your duties in a given day frees you from a crippling feeling of weakness and inferiority. You do not have to lord it over others when you have the inner security of competence and personal strength. What I am talking about here is the substitution of the love of power and authority over your family, friends, and work associates for genuine security in your own competence and a loving intimacy with those around you. When you take the power route rather than the competency-and-love route, you become addicted to playing power games to secure your position among people. You spend more time scheming, plotting, maneuvering, and looking good in the eyes of others than you do in getting an honest day's work done. You live anxiously lest your power connections erode or become unplugged! The more *seeming* success you have at this power search, the more imaginary your personal importance becomes. A facade of your own "godlikeness" begins to form. Soon you may smile and say to yourself, as Friedrich Nietzsche did, "There is no God; if there were, how could I stand it if I were not he?"

To the contrary, when you build your confidence from within through the acceptance of your humanness made possible by the worship of God and not power, you can take or leave the power that comes from around you. When you take it, you use it not only to worship God but to consecrate your strength to God in meeting the needs of people around you, not in manipulating, using, coercing, and lording it over them. The conviction that provides confidence to you and me is that God is God and not ourselves. This helps us to do without facades and masks and *be* the persons we appear to others to be.

The Need to Be an Exception

In the third appeal Satan made to Jesus, he took him to the pinnacle of the Temple at Jerusalem. He told him that if he cast himself down, God would see to it that not even a foot would be struck against stone. He quoted Scripture to prove his point, Scripture from Jesus' own prayer book, Psalm 91:11–12. The angels would catch him before he hit the ground! He would be the exception. He was a privileged character, exempt from the law of gravity.

Being human in our own self-estimate is to confess that we have the same limits all other human beings have. We are not exceptions, not privileged characters, not exempt from the basic laws of creation. The law of gravity is one of these. If we jump off a tower, we are no exception to the law of gravity.

Jesus saw through this hoax. He perceived the offer as a maneuver to put God to the test, to try to corner God early in Jesus' own ministry, to get an absolute assurance that he would be taken care of by God's angels no matter what kind of fool thing he said or did. *He* would not suffer *consequences.* He was different. After all, *if he was the Son of God,* as the devil put it, was he not entitled to this magical protection from all harm? He responded to the devil, "You are not to put the Lord your God to the test" (Luke 4:12, NEB).

In working it out in our own personal wildernesses, we nevertheless ask to be an exception to the common lot of humanity. In a severe illness, we are prone to ask, "Why me, Lord?" Or we may build a paper house of logic that the sole work of God in the universe is to issue exemption slips to us as privileged persons. In our city, the young daughter of a physician was trapped in a whirlpool. In the nick of time someone rescued and resuscitated her. When her father arrived, there was much celebration. Someone said, "Thank God she is alive!" The physician is reported in the newspaper as having said, "If there were a God, she would not have had the accident in the first place." To many people, the main and probably only thing God exists for is to prevent bad things from happening to them. God's job is to set aside the laws of his own creation and not even let us hurt a foot. This is the main girder in this paper house of logic. If you believe this, your confidence in God, in yourself, and in the predictability of the universe will soon be shaken. This illusion is already on its way to disillusionment. Bad things happen to good people, Harold Kushner says (pp. 56–58), because there are "no exceptions for nice people."

> Our human bodies are miracles, not because they defy laws of nature, but precisely because they obey them. . . . But the unchanging character of these laws . . . also causes problems. . . . Laws of nature treat everyone alike. They do not make exceptions for good people or for useful people. . . . A bullet has no conscience; neither does a malignant tumor or an automobile gone out of control.

Therefore, Jesus rejected the fantasy proposed to him by the devil. The Lord our God is not being tested in the labs of the human mind; we are being tested by the impartiality of God's creation. We are called to learn all we can of God's creation and to obey the blueprints of our creation as we grow. You and I will feel our confidence increase as we become disciplined and wise by the things we suffer. As the writer of Hebrews says of Jesus, "Because of his humble submission his prayer was heard: son though he was, he learned obedience in the school of suffering" (Heb. 5:8, NEB). Thus we plant our convictions in the soil of reality and not in the fog of fantasy.

Jesus' Convictions as Your Guide

In these three stressful decisions of Jesus in his wilderness, you and I find our own human nature and its contradictory impulses expressed. In the collision of the perception of the devil with that of Jesus, we see, to use Goethe's phrase from *Faust*, "how force resists and grapples with greater force." As you work out your own personal witness, these three convictions of Jesus will guide you toward a personal image of yourself before God that can stand the wear and tear of dire circumstances. He candidly introduces you and me to the beguiling trickery of our minds in times of success, achievement, and elation. Jesus' wilderness struggles help us to think of ourselves soberly and to increase our capacity to laugh at our fantasies that we are magicians in the face of frustration, successful players in a poker game with the devil, exceptions to all the laws of human nature. They give us a confident serenity when we are frustrated, a spirit of wise discernment when we are flattered by outlandish promises and compliments of others. They provide us a warm sense of fellowship with each other and with our other fellow human beings, regardless of any situation in life.

Whatever else you and I want for ourselves in the quest for bedrock convictions in a fear-ridden world, we do not want to be spectators of Jesus in the wilderness. We do not want to be Holy Land tourists and have some tour guide say, "This is where we think Jesus spent forty days in the wilderness being tempted by the devil." We want to work out our convictions in our own personal wilderness.

Chapter 3

Choosing Whom You Will Serve

Basic understanding of humanness is the wisdom that comes to us in our own personal wilderness. In difficult circumstances we can know our strengths and be clearheaded about our limitations. We learn that each one of us examines his or her own conduct individually. These are some of our responses to being tested. Socrates said, "Know yourself." Contemporary psychotherapists call this "personal insight" or "self-understanding."

Yet if you and I stop here, we are like self-contained ships with nowhere to go. We are on the edge of becoming loners, with no one other than ourselves from whom to learn. We need others in whom we can put our trust—and whom we can safely grow to resemble—without losing our own freedom. We *yearn* to come to know and believe in others as well as in ourselves. Convictions *are* personal, yes; nevertheless, they are validated for us when they are shared. They are blessed when those we love and adore affirm our beliefs by their own words. Their objective "reading" and accepting of us *strengthens* our inner persuasions. Communication with them increases our understanding of our thoughts when those thoughts cease to be simply "in our own heads." As we use words to frame our feelings, those intimations of our private judgment become clearer, more precise, and more easily grasped and remembered.

John Oman, a wise philosopher at Cambridge University in England a generation ago, charted the process of "knowing" the shape of our own most enduring thoughts. He said we know things—particularly the spiritual realities we are convinced enough to commit our whole way of life to believing and doing—in four different ways.

First, *we become aware.* Our five senses—seeing, hearing, touching, tasting, smelling—not only from the physical world around us but also from our inner awareness of our own body and the stored-up memories of our own minds are putting themselves together in ever newer and newer combinations. An idea *strikes* from both without and within. We say, "Hmm!"

Second, Oman says *we apprehend* the object, the idea, the feeling. We concentrate our attention on it. Certain details stand out in the foreground and others arrange themselves around the hot point of attention. We get hold of what it is, or rather *it* lays hold of us. As some people say, "It grabs us!" For example, the apostle Paul, in speaking of his understanding of Jesus Christ, speaks of apprehending or making his grasp of the gospel his own because Christ has apprehended or made him his own (Phil. 3:12).

Third, *we comprehend* the conviction, the truth, the object, the person to whom we have paid our attention. We grasp with our understanding the meaning of that to which we have given our attention. We get wise to what this is all about. We not only get wise; we gain insight. As Proverbs 4:7 puts it, "Get wisdom, and whatever you get, get insight." Again, as the apostle Paul says, "It is my prayer that your love may abound more and more, with knowledge and all discernment" (Phil. 1:9).

Fourth, *we explain* what we have grasped with our understanding. We struggle, as I do now, to put into words for ourself and for someone else what we have experienced. We come to *know* more about what we see, feel, and experience when we wrestle with either writing to or conversing with another person or persons. We develop confidence in what we have seen, heard, handled, and arrived at in our own mind when we clearly put it into words. As the First Epistle of John puts it, "That which was from the beginning, which we have heard, which we have seen with our eyes, which we have looked upon and touched with our hands, concerning the word of life . . . we proclaim also to you, so that you may have fellowship with us."

These are the four phases of the process of knowing according to Oman (pp. 120ff.). I would presume, for our needs here, to add a fifth phase—*we validate.* We share what we have arrived at as true and convincing *for us* with another person or persons. We wait hungrily for a *response.* We hope we are clear and that the response will at least add something to what we understand. We are validated, confirmed, and approved by it. Notice it is no longer just *what* we have said that is appreciated as we are told, "Yes! I understand! I have thought that but never been able to put it into words."

When this happens to you, it is *you* they are accepting, not just what you *say.* The deepest kind of knowing, it seems to me, is in a fellowship of knowing with someone else whose approval is important to you. It arises out of a relationship. This, however, presents a deeper issue: "*Who* is the person whose approval you consider most worthwhile?" You have many persons to whom you relate. Out of the *many* who are important to you, who is the *one* most important of all the rest? Dante, in his *Inferno,* speaks of those "dreary souls . . . who lived without blame, and without praise. . . . They were not rebellious, nor were faithful to God; but were for themselves. Heaven chased them forth to keep its beauty from impair, and the deep Hell receives them not, for the wicked would have some glory over them." In the fellowship of knowing, you are not, as Dante says, just for yourself.

However, there are people who may not yet have considered any persons as important to them. They seem to be at the stage of knowing in which they consider only their own thoughts to be valid. Or some folks prefer to test themselves only by the *things* they have or can acquire, to the exclusion of other *persons*. Their primary loyalty is to things. Or persons themselves may *be* things to other people. You would not be reading this book if these last two kinds of loyalty were habitual for you. You may, though, have suffered at the hands of persons like this. Yet they perform one positive function. They push you and me to be discriminating and careful about *whom* we choose to invest our lives in. They also spur us to challenge their power—limited, finite, and weak as they are—to take over our whole lives. Our awareness, apprehension, comprehension, explanation, and fellowship with others could get locked into them. They do not *have* that power. We *choose* to give it to them.

Challenging the Idols: Having Done with "No-Gods"

When we give finite individuals or groups our worship, they become *idols*. To have an idol means to be unduly obsessed with an object or to *give attentive loyalty to* any object or person less than God. If you and I are to have convictions that give us confidence, we must challenge these idols.

The possibilities of your having been reared and educated in a Christian home, a Christian church, even a Christian college or university are fairly high. Someone has said that the average American spends about five cents out of every thousand dollars on books. I tend to believe that people with a religious background compose a very large percent of that sliver of the book-buying public. Reading is a royal road to Christian privacy, meditation, and personal growth. You are reading this book now. The chances of your being a Christian are very high.

Yet this does not exempt you from the adventure of challenging the idols. Not only in Judaism but also in Christianity, idolatry has always been alluring and appealing. The very lack of confidence you may have in the things you have been taught from your youth up as a Christian represents a passive challenge of what you perceive to be phony, insincere, and even manipulative religious teaching and practice. The apostle Paul saw the pull of idolatry in the Galatians. Before they knew Christ he said that they were "slaves of beings which in their nature are no gods." He found them at that moment—*as Christians*—turning back to these "no-gods," which were "mean and beggarly spirits of the elements" (Gal. 4:8–9, NEB). They were entering the service of idols all over again.

The Great Exchange: How Idolatry Works

The apostle Paul expressed what today we call psychological wisdom in terms of the difference between Creator and creature and what our healthy relationship is. In the same breath he explained how idolatry works in the constriction, oppression, and bondage of a person. This is what the pathological or abnormal personal life is like when we are obsessed with anything less than the worship of the Creator. He said to the Romans that a great exchange takes place. He spoke of those who "exchanged the truth about God for a lie and worshiped and served the creature rather than the Creator" (Rom. 1: 25). The New English Bible translates the word for "exchanged" as "bartered away the true God for a false one."

This, then, is how idolatry works in you or me: we exchange truth for self-deception, deception of others, and God. We exchange the truth of God for a lie. This is *living* a lie, not merely telling a particular falsehood. In his book about the hope for healing human evil, Scott Peck fingers evil as hidden and covert avoidance of the truth about ourselves, our relation to others, and our relation to God. He calls such persons "the people of the lie." When this happens, we give ourselves over to the worship of someone or something less than the God of truth, the Eternal Creator. We worship some kind of creation. From that point on. an idol becomes the organizing center obsessing us.

These idols come in clusters, not easily separated from one another. Some common clusters that we turn to are:

1. Our own selves and personal hungers for food and security, sex and self-assurance of our femininity and masculinity, power and total control of all that affects us, and financial security as it becomes our way of assurance of our self-worth.

2. A lover whose love becomes the center of all we think, do, and are. We can idolize this person and keep her or him on a pedestal; or, in cases of chronic marital conflict, a bitter divorce, a death of a loved one, we can build a hatred-love idol within us that is literally a possession of our spirits.

3. A social position, and all that goes with it—special privileges, slavish dependence on or constant argu-

ments with associates and superiors, the push for climbing the ladder, and the obsessions of profession, political office, and corporate image.

4. A nation or an institution, such as a church, a denomination, a school, a hospital, a company.

5. A particular system of beliefs, such as a theology; a social philosophy such as capitalism or communism; doctrines of infallibility, either religious or scientific.

These are all worthy creations, but they *are* creatures to be assessed, seen for their limitations as well as strengths, and dealt with critically, wisely, and as part processes, not the *whole* of our commitment. When they become our supreme loyalty, when they take the place of God, they are *demonically* possessive. When we let this happen, we begin to live a lie, although we are usually blandly adept at remaining unaware of what we are doing. Our perception naively distorts the world, ourselves, our neighbor, and God. They become to us something they are *not.* As Theodore Roszak puts it (p. 134), "Idolatry is not a moral feeling; it is a mistaken ontology [picture of being], grounded in a flawed consciousness." It is a confusion in our consciousness; we are bedazzled into confusing these creations with the Infinite God.

Let us look more closely at the pantheon of creaturely idols listed above. We can see how easily they enchant us, beguile our minds, and possess our lives. They do not give us a confident rest, as does centered knowledge of and faith in the Eternal God. At the same time, another realization comes to us: The worship of the idol may either make us destructive to others while we pursue our idolatry of ourselves and our hungers or make ourselves sick, distorted, and off-center.

Self-Worship

Browning, in his dramatic poem *Pippa Passes,* tells of a young man named Giovacchino. "He was in violent love with himself, and had a fair prospect of thriving in his suit [for his own love], so unmolested was it." Then a young woman "falls in love with him, too." Then "out of pure jealousy he takes himself off" to another town, never to see her again!

This story makes self-worship ridiculously humorous at the start, but the humor gradually decays, and finally tragedy enters with death in futility. This story also makes narcissism, to use the psychiatric term for self-worship, a predominantly male characteristic. Not so. Women also direct their love upon themselves to idolatrous and destructive extents. Somerset Maugham tells in his novel *Of Human Bondage* about a young male medical student who gave up everything to his own self-destruction in the worship of a self-absorbed woman. Anton Boisen, of whom I spoke earlier as having lived his whole life in focus upon a woman with whom he had failed as a lover, found his way out of his wilderness when he gave himself to a larger loyalty and more Eternal purpose. Women more often will invest primary idolatry into sons or daughters, as does, for example, the mother of a thirty-two-year-old bachelor son who calls him every night at 11:00 P.M. to see to it that he knows she loves him, that he is safe from harm, and that he is really getting ready to go to bed! Who is loving whom?

Worship of Family

Early examples of idolatry include worship of the household gods of Greece, Rome, and Israel, the Great Mother cults, and the fertility cults. Jesus did not want adults to be wholly absorbed by father, mother, brother, sister, and children. He said of his own family, "Whoever does the will of God is my brother, and sister, and mother" (Mark 3:35). This does not mean he did not care for the real needs of his mother, for on the cross he asked his brother-disciple, whom he loved, to care for his mother as if she were his own (John 19:26–27). Yet he steadfastly put the worship of God above family loyalty. He said that we are to leave house and family for the prior claims of the kingdom of God (Matt. 19:29) and for love of husband or wife in creation (Gen. 2:24–25; Matt. 19:4–6). Jesus reminds us that marriage itself is a creaturely relationship, bound by time, space, death; it is not to be idolized as an ultimate, final end in itself. He said that "in the resurrection they neither marry nor are given in marriage, . . . [God] is not God of the dead, but of the living" (Matt. 22:30, 32b). Such realism about the earthly humanness of marriage increases its stability by jarring loose very early some of the idolatrous romanticism of moonstruck lovers and enabling them to love each other as the fragile, error-prone, "in need of forgiveness" beings they are. Jesus' realism cuts away the proud flesh of sentimentality. He reveals the life-giving blood of a down-to-earth woman-man relationship where two people love each other and worship God rather than make idols of each other in exchange for the worship of the Creator. Such human love in the context of faith strengthens marriage by ruling out lies and deception.

Worship of Social Position

As you and I dedicate ourselves to a calling or vocation, however noble or ignoble, these idols gradually shove us onto the competitive social ladder on which we move from one rung to the next. People above us rarely lend a helping hand downward but more often kick us in the face. These "kickers" force us to become fawning "lickers" of their vanity. In turn, those below us are pulling at *our* legs, licking *our* vanity sores for us, and we kick *them* in the face, first, to make them suffer as we did, and second, to keep them from grabbing our place on the ladder. This occurs whether we are in a sacred or so-called secular profession, whether we are in church or so-called secular business, whether we are in church, academic, or state politics.

You can already see the shabby motives of the "licking-up and kicking-down emotions" stirred by the struggle to get and keep a particular social role or position. Free persons do not do this. They see themselves as working with—not under, over, or against—their work associates. But people who make an idol of their positions are not free. They are in bondage. They are obsessed with the infighting of their church, their school, their profession, their political office in government, their place on a hospital staff, or whatever.

This idolatry comes in a cluster with servile dependence upon obsessive hatred of a pastor, a school administrator, another professional to whom a person is answerable, a political superior, or a hospital superior. Deadly games come out of this devilish mix of human passions. People lose their competence in what they are trained to do. They become ill with one or more of a large number of diseases, a common one being clinical depression. The idolatrous construction is the symptomatic rallying center of such illnesses. The person cannot see others except as the not-yet-healed blindman whose eyes Jesus touched a second time. Those with whom one works are seen as trees walking (Mark 8:24). No social position, job, or place is worth this! If you are in such a whirl, think of Abraham, who by faith in God "went out, not knowing where he went." But he had discovered the one true God and had done with idols. He was on his way, by faith, to an enlarged world, to a God who would never constrict his freedom. He recentered the source of his confidence in himself and others by being convinced that the gods around him were no-gods. The God in whom he had placed his faith was eternal and living, not temporary and dying.

For you and me, as for Abraham, this does not happen overnight. Faith that takes such leaps in courage happens again and again over our lifetime, at different stages of our lives. Getting mired down in any one stage prompts us to new idolatries. The process of faith and courage to this growth is similar to the growth of the chambered nautilus, a mollusk of the South Pacific and Indian oceans. The chambered shell grows in two layers. The outer layer is porcelain-like, and the inner one is pearly. As time passes, the shells enlarge the world of the mollusk. Oliver Wendell Holmes describes this in his poem "The Chambered Nautilus."

> Build thee more stately mansions, O my soul,
> As the swift seasons roll!
> Leave thy low-vaulted past!
> Let each new temple, nobler than the last,
> Shut thee from heaven with a dome more vast,
> Till thou at length are free,
> Leaving thine outgrown shell by life's unresting sea!

Worship of a Nation or Institution

Social positions of leadership come and go. Idolizing them comes in a cluster with social institutions of all kinds. Many persons seem to be indifferent to these needs. Rather, they devote a lifelong obsession to the obvious or manifest destiny of the institution or nation of which they are a part. Our churches, the schools where we study or teach, the denominations to which we belong, the hospital staffs of which we are a part, the American nation we love—all these are institutions. We may yield to the temptation to idolize any one or many of them. We overcommit ourselves to them, put them beyond the pale of critical appraisal, and equate all their actions with the very being of God. God is not another Baptist, Presbyterian, Catholic, American, Russian, or any such thing made larger, stronger, and all-inclusive. As Paul Tillich says (p. 13), "The best example of contemporary idolatry is religious nationalism."

The institutional structures of which you and I are a part are not "flat earths" beyond which there is nothing. Before the discovery that the earth is round, before intrepid explorers found sea paths to other continents, the coins of Mediterranean peoples had engraved on them the Pillars of Hercules which stood at the opening of the Mediterranean Sea. Underneath was inscribed the Latin phrase: *Ne plus ultra,* "There is nothing beyond." But after it was learned that there were more worlds than the one they knew, they simply removed the *Ne* and left *Plus ultra,* "There is more beyond." If and when you despair of your institutions, take courage and look for the galaxies of universes God has for you and me to discover beyond these set limits. Isaiah breaks down our idolatry of our own piece of earth when he says:

> Why do you say, O Jacob,
>   and speak, O Israel,
> "My way is hid from the Lord,
>   and my right is disregarded by my God"?
> Have you not known? Have you not heard?
> The Lord is the everlasting God,

the Creator of the ends of the earth.
He does not faint or grow weary,
his understanding is unsearchable.
He gives power to the faint,
and to him who has no might he
increases strength.
Even youths shall faint and be weary,
and young men shall fall exhausted;
but they who wait for the Lord shall renew
their strength,
they shall mount up with wings like
eagles,
they shall run and not be weary,
they shall walk and not faint.
(Isa. 40:27–31)

Worship of a System of Beliefs

A final cluster of appealing idols finds root in our need to fix thoughts and ideas in a final, all-sufficient set of words and statements. These can be in any sphere of thought—theology, philosophy, psychology, biology, chemistry, the whole spectrum of medical science and practice, social philosophies such as communism and capitalism, and many others. In "Idolatry as a Modern Religious Possibility," Emil L. Fackenheim, a Jewish thinker of remarkable insight, speaks of the demonic power of idolatry and challenges the feeling you may have at this moment, that this whole discussion of idolatry is old-fashioned, prescientific, and naive. Fackenheim is critical of a direct transfer of biblical thought about idolatry to modern situations. (I'm sure he would disagree with some of the ways I do that here.) He proceeds to make a case for idolatry as a modern possibility that fits what is happening into the *systems* of today's world. Today, he says, "in the enlightened modern world one is a 'monotheist' if one believes in God or gods at all" (see Donald R. Cutler, ed., *The Religious Situation: 1968,* p. 256). He speaks of the "scandalous particularity of modern idolatry." It cannot be marked off from prejudice or from other sins that are not idolatry. To the contrary, *old* idols are now dead, even though they once had terrifying *power,* and that *power* is still very much alive and has "passed into something else" (p. 269).

Considering systems such as I have mentioned as potential idols, Fackenheim says that we cannot look on them as harmless systems or mere symbols. We imagine we can shear them of their potential, their power, by calling them symbols. To the contrary; they take on a life of their own. They become a final, ultimate religious concern of which the idolater has no consciousness.

Probably the idol most of us are least conscious of is the unconscious assumption that anything we *desire* is entirely possible and a "right" of ours. As Fackenheim says, "The elevation of unlimited human desires to infinite satisfactions *is* the idol." Modern idolatry is the "strange god within" that "desecrates the divine image." Nevertheless, that image must be lived with because God is the Eternal Self within the self of men and women, the infinite within the finite, a distraction the idolater has forgotten or never learned to recognize. The "strange god within" breaks our hearts, sends us on futile races for fulfillment up blind alleys that lead nowhere. The "strange god within" undermines our confidence by sapping the strength from any resolute personal or social conviction that gives us clear goals to pursue.

Willing One Thing: Opposing Idolatry

You can agree with John Calvin about the dark picture of idolatry in the contemporary human mind. As Calvin said (p. 96), "The human mind is, so to speak, a perpetual forge of idols. . . . The god whom man has thus conceived inwardly, he attempts to embody outwardly. The mind in this way conceives the idol, and the hand gives it birth." To oppose this is a kind of warfare. As the apostle Paul says, "The weapons of our warfare are not worldly but have divine power to destroy strongholds. We destroy arguments and every proud obstacle to the knowledge of God, and take every thought captive to obey Christ, being ready to punish every disobedience, when your obedience is complete" (2 Cor. 10:4–6).

To become aware of the idolatry that competes with the knowledge of God in Christ sets up a conscious conflict. This war has been going on unconsciously within us all the time. From this nameless struggle all that has been felt is anxiety, fearfulness, and a lack of confident goal or direction in life. We are "double-minded, unstable in all our ways" (James 1:7–8). To oppose the rending force consciously calls for drastic action on our part. If you and I have had our minds blinded by the gods of this chaotic world, little wonder is it that we see persons "as trees walking." Our capacity to understand has been injured in that we do not *know* ourselves to have "given our hearts away, a sordid boon," to the elemental passions of the no-gods around us. The "strange god within" must become known to us that the perfecting love of God may cast it out. As Paul says, "For it is the God who said, 'Let light shine out of darkness,' who has shone in our hearts to give the light of the knowledge of the glory of God in the face of Christ" (2 Cor. 4:6). When this begins to happen, we renounce self-deception, deception of others, and our desire to be a god or to find one that fits our undisciplined and infinite desiring. We seek a better way to overcome the rift between our idol and the image of God being defaced by it.

A good guide for this open confession is Søren Kierkegaard, the Danish poet and psychologist of the Christian life who lived a brief but creative life of suffering (1813–1855). He called our task the quest for "purity of heart." Purity of heart did not mean to him living a life of puritanical niceness free of mistakes, errors, and sins. It meant singleness of heart, wholehearted commitment to Christ, and unadulterated worship of Christ as Lord. In Jesus' words, it meant to *see* God and to receive the blessedness that comes from purity of heart. Kierkegaard puts it this way (p. 53):

> For only the pure in heart can see God, and therefore, draw nigh to Him; and only by God's drawing nigh to them can they maintain this purity. And he who in truth wills only one thing can will only the Good, and he who only wills one thing when he wills the Good can only will the Good in truth.

Kierkegaard's book, *Purity of Heart Is to Will One Thing,* is a fine tool for thinking through before God your inner uncertainties, tornness, and restlessness. When I read the book I find a collectedness that strips me of noisiness and envelops me in silence, enabling me to become open to my true self and to God. I hope your response will be as valuable to you. The book is devoted to this devout Lutheran's "spiritual preparation for the office of Confession." The following observations from Kierkegaard will help pull away the barriers hindering our vision of God. The observations help us to detect false motives for confession of our manyness, our tornness, our idolatries. We find the price of willing one thing. We see what we must do.

Dealing with Barriers to Willing One Thing

Let me give you the pattern of the discipline Kierkegaard commends to you and to me for clearing our spiritual visions to see the true and living God. It is an intensive self-examination of our motives for relating ourselves to God. This discipline is an intensive opening of the heart before God, "to whom all hearts are open and from whom no secrets are hid" (p. 72).

First, we do not will the Good *for the sake of reward.* To do so "is double-mindedness. To will one thing is, therefore, to will the Good without considering the reward" (ibid.). Rewards are by-products of the vision of God, not the end intention. If they are the motive, we are being tugged at by the "strange god within."

Second, we do not will the Good *"out of fear of punishment"* (p. 79). God is not Santa Claus rewarding us, or a tyrant punishing us. These leave us double-minded. After the gift is received or the punishment is over, the last state is the same or worse than the first.

Third, if we are to come to a genuine vision of God through willing one thing, we must clear up our confusion as to why bad things happen to good people. Are not rewards the consequence of the good we have done, and from God? If not, from where does punishment come to the good? *Where is the justice?* To debate this reminds us of the need of each person to be an exception to the order of nature. Or it can mean our resistance to the discipline of using our intelligence and habits to outwit the suffering that self-indulgence incurs. More deeply, it underestimates the demonic character of evil in an idolatrous world that operates against God. This evil caters to the "strange god within us" with its beguiling promises of utopias in which all our passions will be satisfied completely and we will feel no pain. To oppose this evil is to incur punishment. The German pastor Dietrich Bonhoeffer opposed Hitler's world in which there was "no belief at all. There was a total lack of all serious belief, and in its place [was] make-believe" (Cutler, p. 281). Bonhoeffer chose to live in the real world of God. The make-believe world killed him for it.

Fourth, Søren Kierkegaard speaks of willing one thing only so far, "to a certain degree" (Kierkegaard, p. 104). This is the double-mindedness of *weakness.* Today we would call it hedging on the little things while deceptively professing wholeheartedness on the big commitment to God. It wills the Good weakly. This double-mindedness dwells in "the press of busyness," Kierkegaard says. We appear to have willed the Good, and turn our heads at the small stuff in the way we do business, whether it be in the marketplace, the church, the school, in politics, or in the community. To pause and consider the smaller issues, "to be so scrupulous," seems like "niggardly pettiness" (p. 106). But Jesus said that if "you have been faithful over a little, I will set you over much." We do not commit the grave mistake of a brazen, whole enthusiasm to will the big, no matter whether it be good or bad, says Kierkegaard. This being so, purity of heart does best to focus on the little as well as to hope for the much. These four obstacles to seeing God, then, are to be dealt with decisively in clear ethical and spiritual choices.

The Price of Willing One Thing

The struggle to respond to the call of truth in God to put aside the "strange god within," that we may see God with purity of heart, has its price. The price is, first, commitment "to do all for the Good or be willing to suffer all for the Good" (p. 121). Second, to do this you and I put our cleverness to inward use. A committed person "uses cleverness against himself as a spy and informer, which informs him instantly of each evasion, yes, even gives warning at any suspicion of an evasion" (p. 140). This calls both for taking a stand against evil, as did Bonhoeffer, and at the same time for using our cleverness inwardly to challenge our motivations for taking the stand and our evasiveness in forming our actions.

What Then Must I Do?

How does this take shape in action? Kierkegaard says we are to do three things.

First, we are to *listen* in silence before God, not as a critical theatergoer or as a tourist listens to a tour guide. You and I are being asked, *"What kind of life do you live, do you will only one thing, and what is this one thing?"* (p. 182). Do you truthfully will just one thing?

Second, do you *"live in such a way that you are conscious of being an individual?"* (p. 184). Is the imprint of God or God's own image evident in what you really are according to your eternal vocation so that you are conscious that you are following that vocation? Kierkegaard says, "This consciousness is the fundamental condition for truthfully willing only one thing" (ibid.). This is "the aim of your charge": that your love "issues from a pure heart and a good conscience and sincere faith" (1 Tim. 1:5). This good conscience is the burden of the law of which Jesus spoke and through which Paul said sin works and beguiles the mind to make sin all the more sinful. When we cast down the blind obedience to custom, tradition, and taboos, we are dealing specifically with the "strange god within." We do so as we take up the yoke of Christ and find that by contrast with the Law, it is easy and its burden is light.

The third thing we are to do is to listen to God about our eternal responsibility to be an individual as God asks, *"What is your occupation in life? . . . In your occupation, what is your attitude of mind? And how do you carry out your occupation?"* (pp. 198, 199). Kierkegaard says pointedly (p. 198) that the talk from God

> does not ask inquisitively about whether it is great or mean, whether you are a king or only a laborer. It does not ask, after the fashion of business, whether you earn a great deal of money or are building up great prestige for yourself. The crowd inquires and talks of these things. But whether your occupation is great or mean, is it of such a kind that you dare think of it together with the responsibility of eternity? Is it of such a kind that you dare to acknowledge it at this moment or at any time?

Jesus said that we cannot serve two masters. We "will either hate the one and love the other," or we "will be devoted to the one and despise the other" (Matt. 6:24). In either instance, we will one thing when it comes to choosing what our occupation in life is. By "occupation" I do not mean just how you earn your bread, although that cannot be excluded, but, more completely, the central vocation of your life as an individual, responsible to God for your actions. This *is* your one pearl of great price. You have chosen *not* to cast it before swine, or any "strange god from within." You have searched for this one pearl of purpose; for you it is like the kingdom of heaven. You have found it. You have sold all you have of lesser worth and invested your life in this one thing.

To have such a devotion is to be *called.* To be called in this way is to be convinced and to live life confidently. You know in whom you believe and are persuaded that you are on your way with a strength that is more than your own. That will always be so. Nothing can separate you from it.

Chapter 4

One Clear Calling for You

John Masefield called it sea-fever. He was wholeheartedly devoted to the sea. We see that devotion today in Jacques-Yves Cousteau, who has found in the depths of the sea not only a fascinating universe, with its own inhabitants, colors, and ways of life, but also the expression of his destiny to explore the sea and tell us about it. Masefield described this passionate response when he wrote, in "Sea-Fever":

> I must go down to the seas again, for the call of
> the running tide
> Is a wild call and a clear call that cannot be de-
> nied.

The quest for convictions that strengthen your resolve and mine and start us on a courageous pursuit of life is both an inward and an outward search. To look within, to seek the evasions of your spirit that hinder you, is an inward quest. As you do this, however, you ask, "What is my occupation in life?" This thrusts you on an outward quest to find shape and form, direction and duty for your calling in the world of action. The inner quest is contemplation; the outward quest is action. As Thomas Merton put it, we contemplate and worship in a world of action.

The passion of a high calling urges you to respond to "a wild call and a clear call that cannot be denied" and "go down to the seas again." This calling energizes the timid recesses of your being and brings forth hidden reserves of confidence you did not know you had. Willing one thing from within, in purehearted devotion to God, and responding outwardly to one clear calling as to what you are doing with your life, combine to enable you to stand in the serene courage of your convictions. These two forces merge to intensify each other's strength.

The apostle Paul described his feelings about this inward-outward journey in two statements. He spoke of the inner possession of his ministry as a treasure. He said that he had "this treasure in earthen vessels to show that the transcendent power belongs to God" and not to himself (2 Cor. 4:7). Then he could say of his calling, "I do not consider that I have made it on my own; but one thing I do, forgetting what lies behind and straining forward to what lies ahead, I press on toward the goal for the prize of the upward call of God in Christ Jesus" (Phil. 3:13–14).

When Kierkegaard asks "What is your occupation?" the answer *for you* is given shape in Paul's phrases, "one thing" and "upward call." What one thing calls you upward from whatever your life situation may be now? What under God, and in response to the image of God in you, have you been destined to be and do? This is the main concern of this chapter.

Being Destined and Having a Destination

The first chapter of this book asks the question, "On the fence or on your way?" This question, pushed further, assumes that you have a destination. You are on your way *some-*

where. You have chosen a destination for your life or are in the process of choosing one. Then, having chosen a destination, you are regularly at work correcting your course toward it. You do not drift off course. You have external checkpoints to locate yourself. More than that, you have an internal sense of personal destiny to guide you.

In order to picture in your mind what a sense of personal destiny means, listen to some of the things people around you say in unguarded moments about themselves. One person may say, "Now I know what I was put here to do." Others say, "When I am doing this [whatever the action is], I forget everything else and am all wrapped up in what I am doing," or, "If they didn't pay me to do this, I would be doing it anyhow."

Another way to make the sense of destiny vivid is to read things people have written about it. Walter Rauschenbusch, a German immigrant to America in the nineteenth century, became one of the foremost theologians of the twentieth century. He believed profoundly that the kingdom of God on earth would be brought about by reforms to bring social justice to people who were oppressed, hungry, naked, cold, and without opportunity. He says that when he reached this conviction he found a truth "from which nothing he had ever learned, thought or did was foreign" and to which he could give himself wholeheartedly.

The sense of destiny need not take an explicitly religious shape. Novelist Thomas Wolfe wrote (pp. 577, 587):

> My whole effort for years might be described as an effort to fathom my own design, to explore my own channels, to discover my own ways. . . . I think I know my way. And I shall wreak out my vision of this life, this way, this world and this

> America, to the top of my bent, to the height of my ability, but with an unswerving devotion, integrity and purity of purpose that shall not be menaced, altered, or weakened by any one.

And in an argument with his editor, Max Perkins, who was challenging Wolfe's "way" in a manuscript, he said (p. 588):

> Restrain my adjectives, by all means, discipline my adverbs, moderate the technical extravagances of my . . . exuberance, but don't derail the train, don't take the Pacific Limited and switch it down the siding towards Hogwart Junction.

Wolfe knew that he could be derailed from the track of his destiny. Today, in the era of jet travel and space exploration, we say that we are "blown off course" or are "off the beam" of our radio and radar guidelines. We ourselves, through inattention, preoccupation, or carelessness, can stray off course. Other people, with designs and directions of their own, can seek to divert, reverse, or obstruct our one clear calling. When you and I let this happen to us without a fight, we lose our integrity. The commitment that holds us together has been surrendered. When we are frustrated, diverted, or confused in our destiny by people and conditions around us, our morale drops, our enthusiasm dries up, and we become unproductive. Our performance suffers at whatever task is ours to do.

An overused word for this today is "burnout." Burnout is a set of complaints, signs, and symptoms calling for decisive action on our part to get back on course, to renegotiate, to change our situation so that we are renewed with hope by returning to the inner conviction. Then we are on our way to fulfilling our one clear calling. We are doing and being what we are trained and disciplined to do and to be. We are doing what we were put here to do. The hemorrhaging of meaning and purpose from our life has been stopped. We are being transfused with the lifeblood of new hope. Our energies for living with confident productiveness have begun to return. Our communion with the Eternal within begins to be real once again.

Both personally and as a counselor of others, I know of no one conviction that gives more courage, more zest for living, and more energy for productivity than a clear-cut sense of calling to which you are committed. It has a way of helping you set your priorities in the use of time, energy, and money. You are enabled to sort out trivial matters from matters of great importance by the internal perceptiveness your sense of destiny provides you. In it you have the clearest internal expression of your unique character: who you are, what you are like, how you know yourself to be yourself. Your unique character in turn actively shapes the world around you, stamps itself like a trademark on your work, and influences and persuades other people. It helps you to sort out and accept or reject their influences and persuasions on you. As Walter Rauschenbusch said, it serves as a magnet to bring into proper harmony all that you have ever learned or done.

The growth of a sense of destiny, then, is more than a stroke of fate or luck. As Charles Reade said in the early nineteenth century, "Sow an act, and you reap a habit, sow a habit and you reap a character. Sow a character and you reap a destiny."

A Fixed or a Moving Destiny?

By now you are thinking and asking, "What is my destiny? To what end was I born, and for what purpose am I in the world?" Consider in what manner you have always thought about your sense of destiny in life. One or the other of two major ways of thinking characterizes most people. Which fits you?

Fixed Roles

The first way is to think of your calling, your purpose in life, your destiny in terms of a fixed job or role in life. A role is your part in the drama of life as you live it. Many people consider their role to be fixed, unchangeable, lifelong. They *may* enjoy this; then again, they may feel locked into their role, a prisoner of its demands. One reason for their being locked into a fixed role is that they have learned how to be this way and may fear learning a new way to be. Or they may feel that no matter how many dreams they have of being and doing something different, they are fated to this fixed set of ways of being and doing. There is no use trying to make a dream into reality.

This fixed thinking about people's destiny, what they are "for" in the world, had its uses in agricultural, industrial, and even technological worlds. In the Middle Ages, and to some degree even now, a peasant was born into the world to be a peasant like his or her parents. The land belonged to someone else; the peasant tended it. In some countries today, large corporations and landed families perpetuate this fixed role for the mass of farm families. Farmers raise luxury foods such as coffee, bananas, and tea for distant peoples; they raise very little food and fiber for their own hunger and nakedness. This *is* their fate: a fixed person in a fixed place in a fixed system. One dictatorship is overthrown by another dictatorship, which in turn uses this fixed system for its own self-indulgence. These fixities make a caste system. The caste system sets suffocating limits on the destiny of human spirits. People get sick, stay sick, and die untreated. People get hungry, stay hungry, and die hungry. People rebel in violence and die as a result of violations of human rights. Materialistic messiahs promise them freedom to prosper. They fall for the promise. Then they become the serfs of a new kind of tyranny. Hope turns to blood-drained desperation.

Women and men in the world have both thought of themselves and been thought of by each other as filling *fixed* destinies in life. Freud said of both men and women that "anatomy is destiny." Sexual physiology was perceived as all-determinative, forcing us into cast-iron molds. Women in our time have rebelled at this caste system. Women are indeed mothers; men are indeed fathers. But this does not necessarily mean that women by definition are nurses, secretaries, clerks, and elementary school teachers. Because men are fathers does not mean that men are necessarily the only hunters for food and shelter and money to pay for them. Men are not the only economic burden-bearers. They too can learn to use computers, be effective nurses, and care capably for children. Women in turn can make and repair cars, drive buses, fly planes, be executives. Fixed roles for men and women keep these hidden skills of each from full expression. Without this, the destinies of both women and men are like the gems and flowers of which Thomas Gray wrote in his "Elegy Written in a Country Churchyard":

> Full many a gem, of purest ray serene,
> The dark unfathomed caves of ocean bear:
> Full many a flower is born to blush unseen,
> And waste its sweetness on the desert air.

This darkness and waste happen in any fixed perception of your vocation. As someone has said, the fixed role for the fixed person was a great comfort in another era, but today it is a positive menace both to the individual and to society.

Therefore, let me ask you to reexamine your own perception of your destiny. You are *not* fated and doomed to be just *what* you are just *as* you are from here on out. Regardless of your station in life, you have intelligence that can be disciplined into new acts, habits, skills, and character. Take yourself by the shoulder. Renew your mind. Walk around the circumference of your life and away from your sense of its fixity, fatedness, and unchangeableness. Walk far enough that you see your life as a flowing, growing, ever-changing process. A different angle of vision will present you with inspiration and hope for freedom from a trapped role in life.

A Moving and Growing Sense of Destiny

Both Old and New Testaments use the metaphor of "living water" to picture the flowing, ever-changing, and refreshing nature of life. Dead waters are those that do not move, blend with air, and purify themselves. Without this they become at best "waters of bitterness," at worst, dead waters. This is the way it is with one clear calling. If the calling is one that moves and grows and renews itself in the process, your life is one of adventure, confidence, and renewed strength. Let me be more specific.

Your Vocation and Destiny at the Passages of Life

Elton Trueblood, in his autobiography *While It Is Day,* describes his life as being lived a chapter at a time, a chapter for each stage. As Gail Sheehy has indicated, moving from one of these stages to another is a "passage." Daniel Levinson, in speaking of men, calls them "the seasons of a man's life." As you come from childhood into adolescence, from adolescence into young adulthood, then into middle adulthood, later into maturity and old age, you have both the demand and the opportunity to rechart your course and reassess your destiny in life. This is possible if you see your personal calling as a flowing, living, changing one. However, you are in big trouble if you are a fixed person with a fixed place in life. Let me illustrate.

If you are a parent and see your whole destiny as caring for, attending to, being with, and controlling—"for their own good, of course"—the lives of your sons and daughters, passing time will make this comfortable place in life a miserable prison for you. The reason is plain: Your children cease to need all this caring for, attending to, being with, and controlling. Much earlier than you think, children require less and less parenting. Increasingly, they need you as a source of encouragement, a steadfast fellow adult, an example of how to move out of the single fixed destiny of parenting and into new and adventurous chapters of life. They need you to show them how an adult outgrows one task in life and grows into another. Your life is living water, and you do not stagnate!

Another example is your job. If you see your destiny summed up entirely in the one job you do, even if you have held it for thirty years, your sense of destiny is too fixed for confident living. Institutions, companies, and multicompanies change, whether you do or not. They become outdated, their ideas and equipment become obsolete, they change their personnel, they even go out of existence. You are more confident in your hopes and awareness of your destiny if you continue to learn new skills, master new fields of competence, and equip yourself to meet the needs and demands of the tomorrows ahead of you. For example, I know a career army officer who could easily have stayed in the service until he was sixty or older and been promoted accordingly. However, he decided to write a new chapter in his life. He had had investments and stocks as a hobby for years. He took intensive training in this and became qualified as a stockbroker. At the age of fifty-five, upon completion of thirty years of army service, he started a whole new career and created for himself and his wife a freer schedule and more time together than the army had provided. He and his wife devote much of their freed-up time to their church and to their aging parents. They have a new lease on life.

Then, again, you may be a mother whose children are not out of the home, but are mature high school students. You have always perceived yourself as one who "helps people." Now you would like to become a professional marriage and family therapist. You begin a new period in your life by developing a half-day workday to achieve the professional credentials. It may take you three years to do so, but your son and daughter still need you in the late afternoons and evenings. You *can* do it, and so you do. You have begun a new time of times in the fulfillment of your destiny. Underneath such a change, however, is your willingness to learn new things, your feeling of certainty that you *have* an ever-expanding life calling you, and your hardiness of spirit in staying with a new task until it is done. You move out of a "can't do" mentality into a "can do" attitude.

Retirement is another critical time for older persons whose job has been for all practical necessity their fixed destiny. When your contract runs out by reason of length of service or chronological age, you are tempted to think of yourself as a has-been whose life is over. However, if you see that finishing a certain set of duties and taking up new ones is a lifelong process, this changes your whole perspective of your destiny in life. God is always making things new for you.

Take a look at the numerous things you can do, regardless of age.

A little child quits playing with certain toys. For that youngster they are childish things to be put away. Young children and adolescents, for example, have done with certain modes of transportation. A ten-year-old does not ride a tricycle but a bicycle. A little older and the adolescent ceases to ride a bike; he or she drives a car. In the churches young people go on "youth retreats" (some denominations have "youth revivals"). The time comes, however, when a young person quits this kind of activity. A young adult may moonlight as a waiter or waitress in a restaurant, repair cars, or paint houses to make money while in school. I washed dishes, worked on maintenance crews, and graded papers as a student assistant. I am not above doing any of these things now. However, I have long since given them up as a way to make a living, though the skills remain intact.

What I am saying is that "retiring" starts early in life, usually marks the beginning of a time of newer and more enjoyable skills, and can be a way of life and not the dead end of your destiny. To the contrary, you simply renegotiate your covenant with God and with life to include new assignments that deepen, broaden, and enrich your sense of purpose in creative living. Life flows forward. You flow with it. As you move forward, you accumulate fresh new skills at every stage of your life. These are never laid fully aside. They are assimilated into each new stage in a new form.

From age seventeen to age nineteen I was a weaver in a towel factory. I left that period of my life because I felt called to go to college. Yet I have brought weaving with me all the way to this day. I have never lost a close interest in textures, weaves, and colors of cloth. This interest enriches my conversations with my wife about clothing purchases. I use weavers' figures of speech in teaching and writing. I keep alive my factory knowledge as I counsel with people who work in any kind of factory. The thought forms, values, modes of speech, and ethical code of the blue-collar worker are of intense interest to me. On the wall of my office hangs a "vintage" shuttle of the kind I used as a weaver. A pastoral counseling resident, Drexel Rayford, who devoted two and a half years to working as my younger colleague, is also a musician and composer. He put what I am trying to say into far clearer words than I can. With his permission I share his lyrics with you.

THE WEAVER

With skillful hands
The vagrant threads are woven into bolts.
Separate strands
Of separate hues become a rainbow cloth.

The shuttle moves
And senseless grooves
Find pattern in the plan
That lurks inside
The wary mind;
That is the weaver-man.

And as surely as the finer cloth will last long
    past its time;
As surely as enduring styles won't fade with
    changing minds;
  Surely . . .
In the flowing gowns of princesses
And in the robes of kings,

Are traced the tracks of a shuttle's path
They would be naked, but the weaver sings.

With patient words
Our vagrant moods are woven into sense.
Separate strands
Of broken hearts ride rainbow arcs again.

A shuttle still moves
Through different grooves
And though he's changed his plan;
Weaving words
As grace occurs . . .
For he's still a weaver-man.

And as surely as the finer thoughts will last long
past his time;
As surely as enduring words won't fade with
changing minds;
Surely . . .
When dirty girls become princesses,
As broken men become kings,
We still can trace the shuttle's path;
They would be lost, but the weaver sings.

From a shuttle made of steel and wood to a
shuttle made of grace
His work remains one of weaving . . .
Weaving broken threads of broken lives,
Until every tear's erased.

The shuttle-grace through tender lives
Builds what hope inspires.
In the strengthened cloth of mended hearts,
The weaver never retires.

What I want to convey with this personal story is that you and I in our fulfillment of our destiny are a part of all that we have met. Nothing we have ever done is either an enemy of or alien to our one clear calling under God when we dedicate it to God with thanksgiving and prayer. Each experience becomes a part of the dramatic tapestry of God's unfolding of our destiny. We capture it, weave it in, and keep looking with hope for the new designs God has for our days and years.

Your Destiny and Suffering

Everything up to this point sounds like "smooth sailing" as you realize and fulfill your destiny. At several points, I have mentioned personal discipline. This calls for self-sacrifices and enduring hardships. The beauty of a large, resplendent Tropicana rose in my yard did not just happen. It took heavy work in preparing the soil, careful selection of a healthy plant, much watering during last summer's drought. All this was done for the plant. However, that one beautiful rose represents the pruning of several smaller buds between it and the nutriments of the soil.

Our strivings are not unlike this. Several smaller desires of our lives have to be lopped off. This calls for voluntary choice and endurance of frustration, pain, and even grief if we trim away the many lesser priorities in behalf of willing one thing. Much of the self-help psychology and the human potential reading that we do rarely mentions this factor of personal sacrifice as a normal part of any genuine self-confidence. As a result, much of the recommended serenity of heart is more an external bravado than an inherent assurance. Research psychologist Gardner Murphy speaks of the paradox—a seemingly contradictory but profoundly true pair of truths—of self-realization and self-surrender. He says (pp. 924–925) that it is an ethical necessity that "cannot be banished by shoulder shrugging." He says that we are in "a psychological muddle of big proportions" because we cannot "adjust the paradox." He insists rightly that a human being can be fulfilled and at the same time "so . . . lose himself in others as to care little or nothing about the enhancement of self." Yet Gardner Murphy was confused by this reality.

Suffering and self-sacrifice that are imposed from without are perceived ordinarily as injustice. The same plight that you and I take on ourselves voluntarily and for the loving care of another we perceive as our calling, our commitment. To do so is a joy set before us because of the love we feel for another. Marriages rock and reel for the lack of empathy, self-surrender, and genuine seeking of the marital partner's highest good and greatest happiness. Too often a person wonders what the marriage does "for me." Occasionally, the question is asked, "What can I do to enhance my wife's or husband's fulfillment in life?" Walter Rauschenbusch, in his prayer "For All True Lovers" (p. 94) prayed, "We thank thee for the transfiguring power of love which ripens and ennobles our nature, calling forth the hidden stores of tenderness and . . . overcoming the selfishness of youth by the passion of self-surrender." He might well have said "immaturity" rather than "youth," because selfishness is not restricted to youth, especially in marital conflict.

The inseparability of self-sacrifice from a confidence-giving sense of calling in life is what the cross in human experience is all about. Just as Jesus endured the testings in the wilderness and shows you and me the universal human conditions of our own temptations, his experience of the cross makes clear the way to a life that fears neither death nor life. We are crucified with Christ through faith, as Paul says. *Nevertheless* we live. The life we now live, we "live by faith in the Son of God, who loved us and gave himself for us" (Gal. 2:20). We are continually dying to a self-centered way of life and being raised to a new life of powerful mutual responsibility to those around us. We do not court, cherish, or become enamored of our biological death. Neither do we spend our energies cringing, thinking sadly about, and shaking with fear at the reality that death is to happen to us. Neither do we flirt with death by playing suicidal games. We have already made a decision about death by being crucified with Christ. We live the resurrected life now. Our confidence springing from this conviction is more than psychological self-assurance. It is courage springing from companionship with the earth's most daring son, Jesus Christ.

This is a *daily* discipline of self-surrender. Jesus says in Luke 9:23, "If any [person] would come after me, let him [or her] . . . take up his [or her] cross daily and follow me." Paul says, "I die every day!" (1 Cor. 15:31). If you or anyone else breaks old habits of self-pity, chronic depression, overeating, abusing alcohol or drugs, violent behavior toward a spouse or children, it is not done by a once-and-for-all commitment. We crucify those habits daily. The evil of each day is sufficient. We are given *daily* bread, not bread enough to last us for a lifetime.

Self-sacrifice and Loneliness

Furthermore, taking our lives into responsible discipline like this has benefits. Jesus gave you and me the "open sesame" to the secret of our loneliness when he put the reality of the cross into a brief parable: "unless a grain of wheat falls into the earth and dies, it remains alone; but if it dies, it bears much fruit" (John 12:24). Jesus exposes the loneliness and fruitlessness of the self-centered life. He teaches that we need other people and that the way of the cross—dying daily—leads us to a fellowship with persons who need us and whom we need. Our loneliness is overcome when we break out of our self-centered shells. Andras Angyal, a wise and caring psychotherapist, says (p. 20) that you and I have *two* great hungers.

> We not only have needs, we are also strongly motivated by *neededness*. To be of no use to anything or anybody would make life intolerable. . . . We are motivated to search not only for what we lack and need but also that for which we are needed, what is wanted of us. We struggle to find out what is demanded from us, and we are restless until we find and fulfill these demands.

Finding and fulfilling these demands is the fruit borne by dying to a self-absorbed way of life. Angyal even uses the same thought (p. 240).

> Small wonder that when his neurosis is threatened the person feels that everything is falling to pieces, that he is about to dive into nothingness, that he is dying. Parting with the neurosis feels like parting with life. And indeed one could say, paraphrasing the Gospels, that the patient can gain a new life only by losing his life that is neurotic.

The act of surrender then brings about a new exchange—we exchange the worship of a fictitious, deceptive, and confusing set of false ideals or idols for the worship of the true, self-revealing, and clear-speaking God of our Lord Jesus Christ.

Patterns of Self-sacrifice

When you search for present-day living patterns of sacrificial living after the manner of Jesus, you tend to think of martyrs like Dietrich Bonhoeffer, the German pastor killed by the Nazis; Martin Luther King, Jr., assassinated in his pursuit of racial justice; and Mother Teresa, caring for the poor in India.

Yet if you look around you, evidences begin to appear in the way a certain alcoholic you know died to the old drunkenness and lives a day-by-day resurrected life of sobriety and commitment to helping other alcoholics. A prisoner released from a long sentence becomes dedicated to family, to rebuilding a reputation for work, and to helping other ex-convicts go straight. All around you parents can be found who put their own needs last and their children's needs first. Many negative examples can be found, but these positive ones get no publicity, nor do they seek it.

The Process of Self-sacrifice

The subtle process of self-sacrifice follows a clear design in the actions of your mind and heart. Some of its contours follow.

First, self-sacrifice starts with a deliberate act of imaginative perception. You choose to suspend your own biases, pressing demands, and personal feelings *in order* to perceive the plight of another person from his or her interior world. You intentionally put yourself in the other's situation. You try to think and feel the way he or she does. You practice empathy; you take upon yourself the hurts and hopes, fears and suspicions, angers and feelings of threat that the other feels. For example, as an American, how would I feel about the possibility of invasion by foreign armies if I could remember having been wounded myself and having had 20 million of my fellow Americans killed? That's a little of what it is like to be a Russian today. Or, on personal and less global scale, what does it feel like to be your spouse and to live the life he or she has to live? This kind of imaginative perception enables you to "live considerately with your spouse . . . as a joint heir of the grace of life" (1 Peter 3:7). It just might change your life and your marriage to put your spouse's needs above your own.

Second, the way of sacrifice not only meets your neighbor's needs before your own, not only begins with an imaginative perception of his or her inner world; it moves toward deeper needs of your own than you realized you had. As Angyal said earlier, our lives are restless and insecure as long as we are simply gratifying our more obvious appetites. A deeper hunger to be needed, respected, and loved by that other person is awakened. You reach out for a response of human kinship. Essentially, you do not need or want, as Jesus put it, to "abide alone." Moving sacrificially toward others "connects you up," relates you, and removes your isolation. It frees you from the monotony of staring at a mirror image of yourself. Instead of wasting away in isolation, you thrive in community.

Finally, the way of sacrifice accumulates an invisible and even unknown-to-you treasure of multiplying effects in the lives of people who are influenced by those you serve. Your "tribe increases" without effort on your part but by the capacity of self-sacrifice to beget self-sacrifice in geometric progression. As Paul puts it, "I planted, Apollos watered, but God gave the increase." The long-term return of forgotten acts of self-forgetting you have done in the past ambushes you with surprising joy just when you least expect it. The one clear calling for you, responded to with abandon, validates itself repeatedly in the responses of other people.

Chapter 5

Settling on Your Personal Ethical Code

Codes of behavior are all over the place. Persons and groups have sets of principles and rules by which they live and work. These are codes of behavior. Codes have been written down to be read by all persons since the time of the Code of Hammurabi, written by a king of Babylon who ruled from 1955 to 1913 B.C. The code with which you and I are most familiar is the Ten Commandments. The Bible is a record of many such codes, such as the Deuteronomic Code and many others. Professions today have written and revised codes for the professional responsibility of their members, outstanding among which is the code of the American Medical Association. These are all communal or corporate codes devised by groups and communities of persons.

Our primary concern here is to raise the question: "What is *your* personally chosen code, based on your own experiences as a private human being?" The codes of the Bible *can* and *do* become personally appropriated ways of life. The psalmist speaks of the blessedness of the person whose "delight is in the law of the Lord, and on his law he [or she] meditates day and night" (Ps. 1:2). Even so, such a person also develops individual convictions as to what hard-earned truth is from having collided with the sharp edges of daily living. This can be made more vivid by asking yourself, "What do you do when you know no one is watching you and no one can find out what you are doing?" In your solitude, what is your personal ethical code?

Plato dramatizes this with the story of a shepherd of Gyges, who was tending his sheep one day when an earthquake opened a gash in the earth into which the shepherd fell. At the bottom of this big ditch, the shepherd shook himself free of dirt and looked around. Much to his surprise, he found a beautiful gold ring that fit exactly. Placing it on his finger, he managed to climb out of the ditch and find his way back to his sheep and his fellow shepherds. At the campfire that night, he discovered that when he turned the jewel set in the ring to the inside of his hand, the other shepherds could not see or hear him do or say anything. Later, in the village, he realized that no matter what he did he went undetected by others. He was free of the restraints that others placed on him. As a result, this man, who had previously lived an exemplary life, became an unprincipled thief, a ravager of the persons and properties of others. His previous code was built entirely on what others thought about him. When that no longer was a factor, he had no code except that of the jungle.

Immanuel Kant, the philosopher of Königsberg, East Prussia (1724–1804), raises a similar issue when he supposes (and invites you and me to suppose) that you *alone* know that wrong is on your side. You could confess it, but vanity, selfishness, and the fact that you intensely dislike the person you have wronged (who does not know what you have done) enables you to discard any notion of confession. Only your *respect for yourself* remains. This consciousness of your own personal integrity is all that you have and all that you need, says Kant, in *The Critique of Practical Reason,* to start building your own practical ethic. "When this is well established, when a man finds himself worthless and contemptible in his own eyes, then every good moral disposition can be grafted on it, because this is the best, nay, the only guard that can keep off from the mind the pressure of ignoble and corrupting motives." This calls, as we earlier saw from Kierkegaard, for turning our cleverness inward, cutting away the vanity, the selfishness, and the malice, and building our personal ethical code on the inner core of our integrity before God. As Job said, "Let me be weighed in a just balance, and let God know my integrity" (31:6); "till I die I will not put away my integrity" (27:5b).

Maintaining your integrity in a world of sham is no small accomplishment. Doing so in a churchly world of "sweet, sweet pietism" is just as demanding also. But the confidence it gives you makes it worthwhile. It can be done, but how? Some guidelines I have tested and have seen others test may be helpful to you too. They amount to a code of personal integrity and become convictions in action. To see positive results of your own ethical actions, and to feel your integrity being strengthened, gives you both courage and confidence for facing life unafraid. Let us see what some guidelines for our code are.

Guidelines for Building Your Ethical Code

One reason you and I are chilled by the moral codes current in our day is that they major on minor morals and violate the underlying principles of behavior. As Jesus put it, they are "straining out a gnat and swallowing a camel!" (Matt. 23:24). In searching for guidelines for our ethical code, let's focus on *principles* of relationship, to God and to our neighbor. Then you can unfold the principles in hundreds of specific situations.

The Principle of Mutual Covenants

A covenant is an agreement made up of mutual promises to and from each person making the covenant. Mutuality means a two-way, give-and-take, equally responsible concern and commitment that two or more persons have to and with each other. They mutually respect, communicate with, and take one another into consideration in their actions. Mutuality generates hope in relationships both to people and to God. God's covenants with you and me are always mutual ones. God promises *and* expects. You and I are covenant-making, covenant-keeping, and covenant-breaking beings. If the promises are all on one person's shoulders, the other person is in fact either a helpless infant or is being permitted to behave like one. Except in the case of a real infant, promises made on a one-sided basis run into trouble very early. When you promise like this, you expect gratitude, conformity to your wishes, and control over the other person's life. You expect these things whether you say so or not. When the other person is ungrateful, does not do as you wish, and does not allow you to control his or her life, you become unhappy, lose hope, feel betrayed, and say, "After all I have done for that person, this is the thanks I get!"

Therefore, an imperative code of behavior for me is to see to it that the covenants I make, the agreements I enter, are well balanced and mutual. It is not a selfish thing to put my expectations of the other person into words, clearly and unmistakably. This is far more than a deal that says, "If I scratch your back, you must scratch mine." Reciprocity is the heart of understanding. If you do not have it built in, defined, and clear from the outset of a covenant, you have planted the seeds for later misunderstanding, conflict, and broken relationships. To see to it that your covenants are mutual, then, is to value, cherish, and protect your neighbor as well as yourself. It is ethical love, not just sentimental good intentions.

Furthermore, covenants made and not kept are sure ways of injuring, breaking, or at least bringing to crisis your relationship to the other. Promises must be made very carefully, not lightly, ill-advisedly, or indiscreetly. You know some persons who will promise anything rather than say no. They are "hail-fellow-well-met," likable Joes or Marys who sound far more accommodating than they really are. Yet you know you cannot really count on them. On the other hand, you know persons who promise little and do more. They give you a specific time by which their promise will be fulfilled. You do not have to ask them repeatedly when (and whether) they will do what they said. They are persons you can count on, and they inspire you to be that kind of person also.

The principle of carefully made and mutually kept covenants, then, can be applied in hundreds of situations, the most intense of which is marriage. Your work situation, your church relationships, and your personal friendships are others. These covenants are more than legal contracts, although they have their contractual nature also. Covenants are commitments to faithful function and ethical love, a love always balancing the mutual empathy for and response of persons to one another. The promises we make and keep endear the heart; the promises we make and break, break us apart.

The Principle of Simplicity of Speech

The capacity to speak, to use language, is a powerful source of strength and confidence. With speech we either commune with or confuse others. We reveal, hide, or distort our real selves to those around us. *Simplicity* of speech is the opposite of *duplicity* of speech. I suggest that simplicity of utterance, of the spoken word, reflects our integrity, whereas duplicity confuses others and reveals our double-mindedness. All this becomes very abstract, though, unless we have specific instances to bring it down to earth.

Take "double messages," for example. A person may say to his or her spouse, "I love you, care for you, and don't want to see you hurt, but I'm no longer able to be your husband [or wife]." A teacher says, "You will find this material easy to master, but half the class will fail the course." A father says, "Daddy loves you and wants to be with you, but I've got to go skiing this weekend and can't see you as we planned." Persons listening to this doublespeak are both confused and hurt at the same time. This is duplicity in speech. Simplicity in speech is the opposite. When you speak simply, you give *one* message. Your "yes" is "yes," and your "no" is "no." As Jesus says, "Let what you say be simply 'Yes' or 'No'; anything more than this comes from evil" (Matt. 5:37).

Again, promises made and broken with no attempt to renegotiate them are forms of doublespeak. One of the most prevalent forms of this is procrastination in getting things done that you have promised to do. Being consistently late for appointments is a variation of procrastination. People can only go by what you say you will do. When saying and doing split apart, you have doublespeak, duplicity of speech.

A basic principle of any functional ethical code is simplicity of speech. This puts you to work to get all the double-speak duplicity out of the way you treat others and treat yourself. Character is built in this way. You become a person whose word is his or her bond, whose integrity is counted on by those around you, and an ethical love flourishes in your life. Here again, mutuality generates hope, and relationships are made durable, lasting, and trustworthy.

The Principle of Durability in Relationships

Mutual covenants lay the groundwork for relationships to persons and to God that last, that satisfy the deeper hungers you and I have for security, confidence, and hope. They are day-to-day expressions of the faith in and love for other people and for God by which we live. The apostle Paul says, "There are three things that last for ever: faith, hope, and love" (1 Cor. 13:13, NEB). Therefore, I suggest that durability is a second principle of ethical decision-making. This principle acts in every relationship you and I have to people and to God. When you meet someone new, you gauge non-verbally *how long* the relationship will last as you decide *how much* to invest yourself in the friendship. When you take a job, you ask, "For how long? How much tenure do I have?" When a couple gets married, the words "as long as you both shall live" raise the issue—if they do not settle it!—of the durability of the covenant. Yet, in friendship, work, and love, common sense tells you that you cannot be lastingly related to everybody you meet. Even remembering all their names is a major undertaking. How then can this principle work?

As I have indicated before, the principle of durability works as a guide for discerning *in whom* to invest your time, energy, and other resources. You have confidence for living by reason of your convictions. However, confidence is not just for your private consumption. It is eaten up by the passage of time if it is not invested. As you invest confidence in God and in other people, that confidence is increased in strength, value, and clarity. Yet you need a measure by which to discern the kinds of people who are trustworthy and who in turn are concerned about the lasting quality of their relationship to you. Durability is a measure for these decisions being made. Some persons are casual, superficial, and even flippant about sustaining relationships with others. They contact people for their own uses; they do not relate durably to them over time. Other people have an intuition of the Eternal in the ordinary meetings with others in the marketplace, the shops, the factories, the offices, the classrooms, the churches, the political meetings, and in the home. If they sense that you, too, have an eye and a heart for the Eternal in your care for other people, you "correspond," you "resonate," you "vibrate" with them.

Relationships so formed start on bases that assure they will last. They tend to form slowly. They are not instant intimacies in a short-order "use" of persons. They are steadfast in their growth over time.

As I consider friends I have known and worked with over twenty, thirty, or forty years, I know these relationships have been marked by high regard for one another, a deep sense of empathy (that works in both directions) and a fierce refusal to use and abuse each other for short-term gains. These friendships have been proven and tested over the years by crises we have suffered together. For example, my friend of forty-seven years, Henlee Barnette, the author of the book *Your Freedom to Be Whole* in this series of Potentials, endured the Vietnam War with me. At the same time as my elder son,

Bill, spent twenty months in the Naval Riverine Assault Group, one of Henlee Barnette's sons spent two tours of duty as an intelligence officer in the Air Force. His other son at the same time refused to be drafted and stayed in Sweden four years. We struggled daily in agonizing prayer together. Every fiber of our character was tested. Our faith in both humankind and in God was under fire. Yet ten years have put it behind us, and we can affirm with James 1:3 that "the testing of your faith produces steadfastness."

The principle of durability, then, could also be called "steadfastness"; that is, "standing hitched together when the going gets roughest." Yet the maintenance of steadfast relationships calls for another principle or guideline for our ethical code. That is the daily discipline of face-to-faceness in human relationships and in relationship to God.

The Principle of Day-to-Day Face-to-Faceness

If you and I have lasting relationships to others, we maintain those relationships by knowing each other on a face-to-face basis. A quaint phrase from my hill-country heritage in western South Carolina says this well. People said, "I haven't laid eyes on him [or her] for too long." My grandmother would say to me when I had been away a long time, "Come here to me and let me lay eyes on you, my grandson." This tender intimacy was given a Christian meaning by Thomas Helwys in one of the Free Church confessions of 1612. He said that "the members of every church or congregation ought to know one another, that so they may perform all the duties of love to one another both to soul and body."

Yet maintaining face-to-faceness is easier said than done. People offend one another, both intentionally and unintentionally. People sin against each other with a high hand, and not just unwittingly. People get hurt. They withdraw from each other. They "never want to lay eyes on each other again." People refuse to be reconciled to each other. They live in the mistaken fantasy that human relationships *can* be ended, when in reality they can only be changed from good to bad, bad to worse, worse to impossible. Yet, with courage and conviction, persistence and patience, such relationships can be restored.

If they are kept in good health or, in the case of severe conflict, restored to well-being, then the hardest but surest way of doing so is through face-to-face meeting, renegotiation, mutual awareness, and confession of error. If you have been offended by someone, your first temptation is to say so to everyone *but* that person. Each time you tell the story, it gets exaggerated just a bit more than the last time you told it. These stories get back to the one who has offended you. He or she talks to everyone but you. There are a few people in these two sets of "everyones" who *like* to see you and the other person fight. The first casualty of this process is your face-to-face meeting with the one who has offended you.

The sayings of both Jesus and Paul give the surest guide to ethical living here. Jesus said, "If one of your fellow believers sins against you, point out the fault privately just between yourselves. If your neighbor listens to you, you have gained your neighbor" (Matt. 18:15, adapted). This is the place to start. The objective is to open the other's ears to hear you, to be heard. The apostle Paul gives an additional angle of vision: "Even if a man [or woman] is overtaken in any trespass, you who are spiritual should restore him [or her] in a spirit of gentleness. Look to yourself, lest you too be tempted" (Gal. 6:1). The person who fretted you may be carrying a personal burden about which you are not aware, and has certainly created a burden for you to carry. If you approach that person with a spirit of gentleness, each of you is more likely to be able to bear the other's burden.

If you adopt these instructions of Jesus and Paul as your personal code, you will, as Jesus predicted, be able to gain your neighbor [brother or sister] in many cases. Other cases fail and require that you try again and take a third reconciling person with you. This also has successes and failures, but it is worth the effort. Yet this kind of directness and face-to-faceness is a rare thing even in religious circles. We live behind masks of niceness, piety, and spiritual pride that are not easy to remove for such candor and forthrightness. Middle-class people are terrified at such face-to-faceness at first, accustomed as we are to criticizing people behind their backs and soft-soaping them to their faces. However, making this a part of your code will in the long run give you a stronger integrity and maintain other people's respect. You will not win in all instances, but you have been faithful. Stand and wait for life itself to change things. It often does.

To adopt face-to-faceness as your code is to enter the ethical sphere of life by the narrow gate where the way is hard, but it leads to life, not destruction. Wider and easier ways are everywhere.

The Principle of Greatness of Heart

The principle of face-to-faceness can become a "flamingo ethic" if it is followed to the exclusion of other principles of an adequate code of life. The flamingo is a bird native to parts of Europe and the extreme southern parts of the United States. When you drive through swamplands of Florida and Louisiana, you often see these birds in their splendid beauty, standing on *one* leg. Many ethical codes stand on one principle just like that. Face-to-faceness can take the ethical imperative of encounter to the absurd. You can "stand people down" over trivial things that could best be dealt with by ignoring or never mentioning them, or mentioning them only to your spouse or other confidant. Those trivial things are not worth the breath it takes to recount them.

To be able to do this calls for another ethical principle—that of greatness of heart, or magnanimity. This is the opposite of meanness of spirit, little-mindedness, and vengefulness. Greatness of heart, or magnanimity, is not a goody-two-shoes namby-pambiness. It is far more than a set of good feelings, real or contrived. Greatness of heart has at least three psychospiritual ingredients necessary for living productively.

First, greatness of heart consists of a *perspective* of the smallness or greatness of an event, an offense, or an issue. Large events, offenses, and issues are met firmly and courageously, but gently. Small ones are overlooked, disregarded, and ignored. They are treated with benign neglect. Even if they are noted, nothing is made of them. A greathearted perspective is fueled by the spirit of discernment whereby you, being mature, have trained your faculties to distinguish good from evil, the significant from the insignificant, the trivial from the intensely important.

Second, greatness of heart, or magnanimity, is inspired by having *convictions* in which you are confident. You are secure in your own integrity and are not thrown off balance by every petty action of others. You are guided by a North Star, your own ethical compass and sextant, and balanced by the inner gyroscope of your relationship to God. You are not blown off course by the bluster of others, nor do you drift astray by not paying attention to who you are and where you are going.

Third, greatness of heart and magnanimity are nurtured by the *sense of awe and wonder.* Immanuel Kant said, "Two things fill the mind with ever new and increasing admiration and awe, the oftener and the more steadily we reflect on them: the starry heavens above and the moral law within."

I have spoken here of only a few principles of an effective ethical code. As you reflect on the grandeur of the starry heavens above you and the moral law within you, add to my reflections your own additional principles. A growing ethical code is open ended. It can encompass emerging principles not yet revealed to us by which we can live, courageously and with certainty, in a nuclear and hazardous world by glorifying God and enjoying God forever.

Questions for Thought and Discussion

1. What major hindrances get in your way when you are faced with making an important decision?
( ) The spiritual air you breathe? ( ) The illusion of perfect self-fulfillment? ( ) A wounded capacity for commitment? ( ) Lack of and need for accurate information?
( ) Other?
Specify.

2. What is your personal wilderness?
( ) An impossible job? ( ) A continually denied desire?
( ) Being trapped in an unworkable marriage? ( ) Being isolated in a rural area, city, or foreign land? ( ) Other?
Specify.

3. What is your greatest temptation to idolatry? (See pages 57–58.)
( ) Cluster 1? ( ) Cluster 2? ( ) Cluster 3? ( ) Cluster 4? ( ) Cluster 5? ( ) Other?
Specify.

4. If God granted you the opportunity to do with your life what you most fondly dream of doing, what would it be? What skills would you need to learn?

5. Write your own personal ethical code. Wherein does it differ from what people around you expect of you?

Selected Bibliography

Angyal, Andras. *Neurosis and Treatment: A Holistic Theory.* John Wiley & Sons, 1965.

Boisen, Anton. *The Exploration of the Inner World.* University of Pennsylvania Press, 1936.

Calverton, V. F., ed. *The Making of Society.* Modern Library, 1937.

Calvin, John. *The Institutes of the Christian Religion, I.* Wm. B. Eerdmans Publishing Co., 1957.

Cutler, Donald R., ed. *The Religious Situation: 1968.* Beacon Press, 1968.

Dowling, Colette. *The Cinderella Complex: Women's Hidden Fear of Independence.* Simon & Schuster, Summit Books, 1981.

Kierkegaard, Søren. *Purity of Heart Is to Will One Thing: Spiritual Preparation for the Office of Confession,* tr. by Douglas V. Steere. Harper & Row, Harper Torchbooks, 1956.

Kiley, Dan. *The Peter Pan Syndrome: Men Who Have Never Grown Up.* Dodd, Mead & Co., 1983.

Kushner, Harold. *When Bad Things Happen to Good People.* Schocken Press, 1981.

Murphy, Gardner. *Personality.* Harper & Brothers, 1947.

Neill, Stephen. *A Genuinely Human Existence.* Doubleday & Co., 1959.

Oman, John. *The Natural and the Supernatural.* London: Cambridge University Press, 1950.

Peck, Scott. *People of the Lie: The Hope for Healing Human Evil.* Simon & Schuster, 1983.

Rauschenbusch, Walter. *Prayers of the Social Awakening.* Boston: Pilgrim Press, 1910.

Roszak, Theodore. *Where the Wasteland Ends: Politics and Transcendence in Postindustrial Society.* Doubleday & Co., 1972.

Tillich, Paul. *Systematic Theology, I.* University of Chicago Press, 1951.

Wolfe, Thomas. *The Letters of Thomas Wolfe,* ed. by Elizabeth Nowell. Charles Scribner's Sons, 1956.

Yankelovich, Daniel. *New Rules: Searching for Self-Fulfillment in a World Turned Upside Down.* Bantam Books, 1981.

Notes